THE ATLAS OF
ENDANGERED SPECIES

Richard Mackay

Earthscan Publications Ltd, London

First published in the UK in 2002
by Earthscan Publications Ltd

A catalogue record for this book is available
from the British Library

ISBN: 1 85383 874 8

Produced for Earthscan Publications Ltd by
Myriad Editions Limited
6–7 Old Steine, Brighton BN1 1EJ, UK
http://www.MyriadEditions.com

Edited and co-ordinated for Myriad Editions by
Jannet King and Candida Lacey

Design and graphics by Corinne Pearlman
Maps created by Angela Wilson,
All Terrain Mapping, Fareham, Hants, UK
Additional research by Jannet King

Printed and bound in Hong Kong
Produced by Phoenix Offset Limited
under the supervision of Bob Cassels,
The Hanway Press, London

For a full list of publications please contact:

Earthscan Publications Ltd
120 Pentonville Road, London, N1 9JN, UK
tel: +44 (0)20 7278 0433
fax: +44 (0)20 7278 1142
email: earthinfo@earthscan.co.uk
http://www.earthscan.co.uk

Earthscan is an editorially independent
subsidiary of Kogan Page Ltd and publishes in
association with WWF-UK and the International
Institute for Environment and Development

CONTENTS

IUCN Categories

The following categories are used throughout the book. For further details see:
<www.redlist.org/info/categories_criteria.html>

Critically endangered – A taxon is critically endangered when it is facing an extremely high risk of extinction in the wild in the immediate future.

Endangered – A taxon is endangered when it is not critically endangered but is facing a very high risk of extinction in the wild in the near future.

Vulnerable – A taxon is vulnerable when it is not critically endangered or endangered but is facing a high risk of extinction in the wild in the medium-term future.

Evolutionary adaptation has given rise to a cornucopia of life. Of all the species that have ever lived, only a tiny fraction are alive today. Spasms in the Earth's history, caused by volcanoes erupting and meteorites impacting, have wiped out entire groups of organisms, and gradual climatic changes have eliminated others. The evolutionary strategies of some species were just not good enough and they succumbed to competitors and predators. The demise of the dinosaurs is a humbling tale. Their awesome size and power did not assure their survival. Quite the reverse: it left them slow to adapt to a changing environment and more vulnerable than mammals to catastrophic events.

As humans, the psychological trap of believing ourselves to be a class apart from other creatures is exacerbated by the absence of other living hominids. The Australopithecines, Homo ergaster and our other ancestors took tools, organization and culture well beyond the level of sophistication of primates. Although we are of their line, the biological changes that accompanied their advance are sufficient for us to consider ourselves a different chrono-species.

Some parts of the world are more ecologically interesting than others. Habitats such as coral reefs and rainforests contain a great variety of species. Some intrigue us because, like the Arctic and Antarctic, their wildlife is peculiar and we have not yet heavily disturbed them. Species on islands such as Madagascar developed in geographical isolation, giving rise to unique forms. Australia has the dubious distinction of the most mammal extinctions. Many other regions and ecosystems are worthy of study but limited space precluded descriptions of them in this book.

A small fraction – probably fewer than ten percent – of living species have been identified and classified. The remaining 90 percent are mostly plants and invertebrates. Consequently, the anomaly arises that countries that have been most intensely researched show up as having the highest number of threatened species. The World Conservation Monitoring Centre, now a division of the United Nations Environment Programme, is the global data organization for conservation. IUCN-The World Conservation Union is the umbrella group for conservation bodies around

the World. IUCN has promulgated a system for assessing whether a species is threatened and, if so, the severity of the risk. The definitive work is the organization's publication, *2000 IUCN Red List of Threatened Species.*

Representing the number of species threatened endorses the notion of a species as a closed gene-pool. This presents conceptual difficulties, such as in defining species among organisms that are "parthenogenetic" – they produce offspring from unfertilized eggs. Despite its flaws, however, the species concept is useful for conservation. Subspecies and isolated populations of species are not counted in this book, although they are sometimes described in the text.

The distribution of living things does not respect political boundaries. However, decisions affecting conservation are still usually made by states and their borders provide a convenient means of dividing the land surface. For groups of animals and plants, the level of threat has been represented in this atlas by the number of threatened species occurring in each country. This inevitably gives the impression that larger countries have greater conservation problems than smaller ones. To redress the balance, Part 6 "Issues of Conservation" highlights areas with the greatest biodiversity and those with the most endemic species.

Why should conserving biodiversity matter? Apart from aesthetic loss, each extinction also represents the loss of irreplaceable genetic information, including beneficial characteristics that could have been bred into domestic crops and livestock. Chemicals produced naturally are also used to develop pharmaceuticals. When "keystone" species become extinct the balance of whole ecosystems is threatened.

Agreement between states can secure the conservation of common resources, such as ocean fisheries. It can also suppress damaging wildlife trade, driven by our fascination with the rare and exotic and the purported medicinal properties of some plants and animals. The Convention on International Trade in Endangered Species of Wild Fauna and Flora (CITES) was adopted in 1973. More recent treaties have addressed conservation within national jurisdictions. In 1992 the United

Nations Conference on Environment and Development in Rio de Janeiro (the "Rio Summit") adopted the Convention on Biological Diversity, the Convention on Climate Change and Forest Principles. All are relevant to threatened species. Although the Convention on Biological Diversity restated the principle of national sovereignty, it also placed a duty on states to conserve biodiversity by requiring that environmental impact assessments be carried out for infrastructure projects, for example.

The size of the human population is of major consequence in conserving biodiversity. Fewer people would allow us to leave habitats intact or to exploit them sustainably. Of course the environmental impact, or "footprint", of individual countries differs. The USA, with 4 percent of the world's population, produces a quarter of the world's greenhouse-gas emissions. However, the USA and other industrialized countries also produce most of the world's clean technologies.

Modern pollution is a global issue. Carbon dioxide warms the whole planet, not just your back yard. The impact of global warming on threatened species will be profound. Polar bears will be stranded and starve as ice retreats. Plants with a limited distribution may not survive rising temperatures. Coasts and estuaries will be inundated. The world will lose natural species that have evolved over billions of years to form communities and habitats that without human interference would still exist in exquisite equilibrium.

The Convention on Climate Change went to the very heart of economic systems. An accord was signed in Kyoto in 1997, outlining binding limits on the global warming contributions of developed countries. The extent to which the transfer of clean technology to developing countries and "carbon sinks" could be debited from national emissions was contentious. In November 2000 talks in The Hague, Netherlands on the detail of the Kyoto agreement foundered on US intransigence, but in July 2001 a compromise agreement was reached by 180 countries (excluding the USA). It is hoped that this represents a significant first step towards concerted international action on global warming.

My thanks go to Patricia Patton at WWF-UK, and to Alex Solyom at WWF-US, who kindly supplied most of the photographs included in this book, and to the photographers who have generously given us permission to use their images in this atlas. (See opposite for full photo credits.)

I would also like to thank the Species Survival Commission of IUCN and Birdlife International, who were both helpful in clarifying data.

I am very grateful to the team at Myriad Editions – Jannet King, Candida Lacey and Corinne Pearlman – who worked tirelessly to ensure the rigor and visual impact of the book, and to the cartographer, Angela Wilson.

Another sincere acknowledgement is to my mother Judith, who proposed that I take on this project and, with my father John, gave her wholehearted support during its evolution. Finally, deepest thanks are due to my wife Kate, without whose wonderful encouragement the book would not have been written.

RICHARD MACKAY
Cambridge, UK
July 2001

Richard Mackay and Myriad Editions are grateful to WWF in the USA and UK for permission to use a selection of images from the WWF photo archives. Known worldwide by its Panda logo, WWF is one of the largest and most accomplished international conservation organizations. With offices or resident representatives in more than 50 countries and field projects in more than 100 countries, WWF is working across the globe to protect endangered species and to save endangered spaces.

To learn more about WWF and its programs, visit the organization's portal website at <www.wwf.org>. WWF assumes no responsibility for the accuracy of the text, maps or charts in the atlas.

10–11: Giant tortoise, Neil Morrison WWF-UK
18–19: Neanderthal skull, Patrick McDonnell/ www.medicalillustration.net
20–21: Red Sea coral, Charles Hood/WWF-UK
22–23: Mahogany tree, Brazil, Mark Edwards/Still Pictures/WWF-UK; Tropical forest, WWF-UK; Rainforest destruction, Indonesia, Mauri Rautkari/WWF-UK
24–25: Forest fires, Russia, Per Angelstan/WWF-UK; Illegal logging, China, Stuart Chapman/WWF-UK
28–29: Okavango, Botswana, Chris Harvey/WWF-UK
30–31: Mangroves, Edward Parker/WWF-UK
32–33: Red Sea coral, Charles Hood/WWF-UK
34–35: Atlantic forest, Edward Parker/WWF UK
36–37: Polar bears, Neil Morrison/WWF-UK
38–39: Macaroni penguins, Mary Rae/WWF-UK; Rockhopper penguin, David Lawson/WWF-UK
42–43: Muriqui, Luiz Claudio Marigo/ www.omuriqui.hpg.com.br; Atlantic forest burning, Edward Parker/WWF-UK
44–45: Steven Morello/WWF-US; Lava gull, Gary Feldman/ feldman@physics.harvard.edu; Giant tortoise Neil Morrison/WWF-UK
46–47: Madagascar rosy periwinkle, David R. Parks/www.mobot.org; Fish eagle, Greg Lasley/ glasley@earthlink.net; Golden bamboo lemur, endangangeredcreatures.net
48–49: Cheetah, Chris Harvey/WWF-UK
50–51: Gorilla, Rick Weyerhaeuser/WWF-US; Drill monkey, D. White/WWF-UK; Alaotra gentle lemur, David Lawson/WWF-UK
52–53: Florida panther, David Maehr/Conservation Biology, University of Kentucky, www.fl-panther.com; Cheetah, Chris Harvey/WWF-UK; Bengal tiger, David Lawson/WWF-UK

54–55: Bison, USFWS/WWF-US; Przewalski's horse, John De Meij/Foundation for the Preservation and Protection of the Przewalski Horse/ www.treemail.nl/takh; Hunter's hartebeest, Gretchen Goodner/WWF-US
56–57: Indian elephant, David Lawson/WWF-UK; Indian rhino, Bruce Bunting/WWF-US
58–59: Brown bear, Mary Rae/WWF-UK; Spectacled bear, David Lawson/WWF-UK; Giant panda, Edward Mendell/WWF-UK; Asiatic black bear, Ian Ledgerwood/WWF-UK
60–61: Beaver, David Lawson/WWF-UK
64–65: Blue whale, Paul Coppi/WWF-UK
66–67: Marine iguana, T. P. Littlejohns/WWF-UK; Asian three-striped box turtle, Kurt Buhlmann/ Conservation International
68–69: Monarch butterfly, WWF-US
70–71: Aquaculture, Edward Parker/WWF-UK
72–73: Lady's slipper orchid, E. Lister/WWF-UK; Wild bluebell, Michael Steciuk/WWF-UK; Caucasus, Cathy Ratcliff/WWF-UK; Bastard quiver tree, Craig Hilton-Taylor/IUCN Red List Programme; Mandrinette, Wendy Strahm/IUCN Red List Programme
74–75: Short-tailed albatross, Hiroshi Hagesawa/Toho University
76–77: Kiwi hen, Storm Stanley/WWF-UK
78–79: Great Phillippine eagle, www.phillipineeagle.org
80–81: Spix's macaw, Tony Pittman/ www.bluemacaws.org; Yellow-eared conure, Paul Salaman/Proyecto Ognorhynchus; Hyacinth macaw, Edward Parker/WWF-UK; Female Mauritius parakeet, Anne Lee/WWF-UK
82–83: Short-tailed albatross, Hiroshi Hagesawa/Toho University
86–87: Epiphytes, Russel Mittermeier/WWF-US
88–89: Chimpanzee, David Lawson/WWF-UK; Red ruffed lemur, David Lawson/WWF-UK; Galapagos tortoise, Charles Hood/WWF-UK
90–91: Rainforest, Sumatra, Mauri Rautkari/WWF-UK; Epiphytes, Russel Mittermeier/WWF-US Pa-hay-okee, Hugh Clark/WWF-UK
92–93: Pygmy hippo, David Lawson/WWF-UK; Golden lion tamarin, David Lawson/WWF-UK
96–97: Golden pagoda, Craig Hilton-Taylor/IUCN Red List Programme
98–99: Angler sattelschwein/FAO; Red Maasai sheep/FAO
100–101: Orang-utan, Russel Mittermeier/WWF-US
104–105: Monarch butterfly, WWF-US

Terrain bases on pages 26–27, 36–37, 38–39, 40–41, 43, 46–47 and 92–93 were prepared using MAPS IN MINUTES™ © RH Publications (1999).

EXTINCTION IS FOREVER

1

"Pragmatic self-interest alone should teach us that
we must change before nature exacts inevitable revenge."

— David Watson,
author of *How Deep is Deep Ecology*

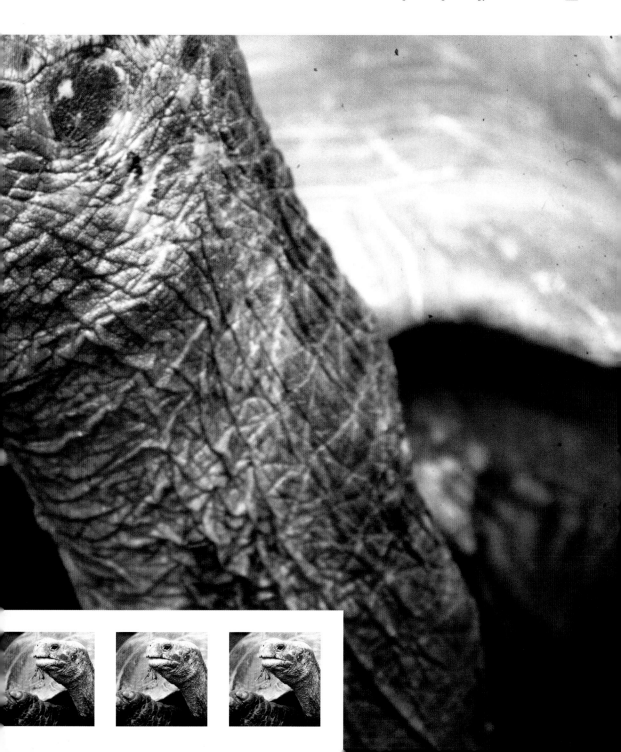

EVOLUTION

In 1831 the British naturalist Charles Darwin took a fateful voyage on the survey ship HMS *Beagle*. Over five years he studied the geology and wildlife of the lands the *Beagle* visited. He found fossils of species long extinct and wondered how new species had replaced them. His observations led him to deduce that the difference between species was an outcome of natural processes. Darwin's thesis culminated in the publication in 1859 of *On the Origin of Species*. Here he challenged the prevailing orthodoxy that the diversity of life was the product of supernatural design.

By Darwin's day the concept of a "species" was widely understood as a group of organisms that can breed with each other but cannot interbreed with another species. The Swedish botanist Karl von Linné (who became known by his Latin name of Carolus Linnaeus) had developed a system in the mid-18th century that classified organisms according to their similarities, placing them in a hierarchy that, at the highest level, makes the basic distinction between animals and plants. His approach forms the basis of modern-day taxonomic diagrams (see opposite).

The difference between the approach of Linnaeus and Darwin was that while Linnaeus saw his work as "mapping" the world God had created, Darwin was interested in explaining how living creatures evolved and continued to develop. Darwin observed that there is variation within a species and that some characteristics are more beneficial than others. He knew that the characteristics of an adult organism depend on its parents and the environment where it lives. As life is a competition for scarce resources and a test of resilience in the face of harsh conditions, organisms with characteristics most likely to allow them to survive will breed most successfully. Those characteristics will then become more prevalent within the species as it adapts – or evolves – to its changing circumstances. When events such as a rising sea level or the movement of the Earth's continents splits a population into two, the new populations cannot meet to interbreed. Over time, separate evolution will cause changes in each group to the point where they can no longer successfully reproduce with each other – a new species has evolved.

A taxonomic diagram, such as the simplified version opposite, relates species by their evolutionary history. Species of the same order are considered to share a more recent common ancestor than species of the same phylum. Different species with similar features are grouped into families. Similar families belong to an order, related orders to a class and classes to a phylum, each of which belongs to one of the kingdoms. There are, however, different criteria for assigning organisms to different groups, and continuing debates as how the divisions should be made, even at the highest level of the kingdom.

Darwin's theory of evolution is itself constantly being reviewed. In the 20th century scientists studying life at the molecular level recognized that natural selection occurs only indirectly between whole organisms (animals and plants). At a more fundamental level it is occurring between genes. This explains behaviors such as altruism: for example, ants will sacrifice themselves to defend their nests because what is important is the survival of the genes shared by related ants rather than survival of the individual.

EVOLUTION SIMPLIFIED
How a single species can evolve into many species

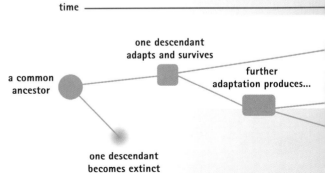

time

one descendant adapts and survives

a common ancestor

further adaptation produces...

one descendant becomes extinct

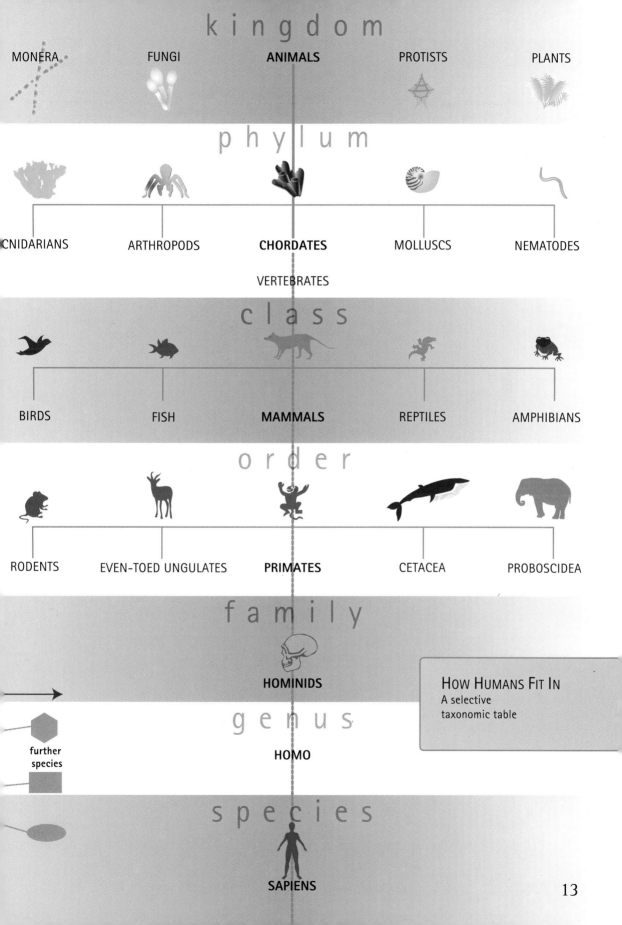

kingdom

MONERA   FUNGI   **ANIMALS**   PROTISTS   PLANTS

phylum

CNIDARIANS   ARTHROPODS   **CHORDATES**   MOLLUSCS   NEMATODES

VERTEBRATES

class

BIRDS   FISH   **MAMMALS**   REPTILES   AMPHIBIANS

order

RODENTS   EVEN-TOED UNGULATES   **PRIMATES**   CETACEA   PROBOSCIDEA

family

HOMINIDS

HOW HUMANS FIT IN
A selective
taxonomic table

genus

further
species

HOMO

species

SAPIENS

13

MASS EXTINCTIONS

The "biodiversity" of a place or region is a measure of the number of species present and of their abundance. Each species occupies a "niche" – a specific location, relationship with its physical surroundings and mode of interaction with other species. Organisms of a single species in one place are called a population, and together populations form a community.

Species naturally become extinct as they fail to reproduce, either through extreme conditions or because of displacement by competitors. Even if a species adapts to these threats, it will, by definition, have evolved into a different species. Fossils suggest that this background rate of extinction is punctuated by short periods of mass extinction, defined as a period in which at least 50 percent of all species become extinct.

The precise cause of each mass extinction is difficult to assess. Catastrophes such as meteorite impacts and comet showers may have been responsible for some mass extinctions. Global climate change, fluctuation in the concentration of various gases, and other gradual environmental trends may have caused others.

Interactions between species could even have been a factor, creating instability in complex, finely balanced communities. The loss of certain "keystone" species can be particularly damaging to communities. For example, in areas where otters have recently been hunted nearly to extinction, sea urchins have multiplied, consuming the kelp and so radically altering the habitat. Keystone species may be as small as soil invertebrates or even microbes.

Mass extinctions overwhelmed creatures living both on land and in the sea. On land, animals seem to have suffered more than plants. In the sea, trilobites – a group of marine animals with hard shells – have suffered a repeated loss of species.

Mass extinctions have occurred roughly every 26 million years. It is not clear if this pattern has arisen by chance, or whether there is some explanation for it. There have been five particularly widespread mass extinctions. The species that survived, subsequently diversified to occupy the niches vacated by those that vanished. Thus, new forms of life appeared.

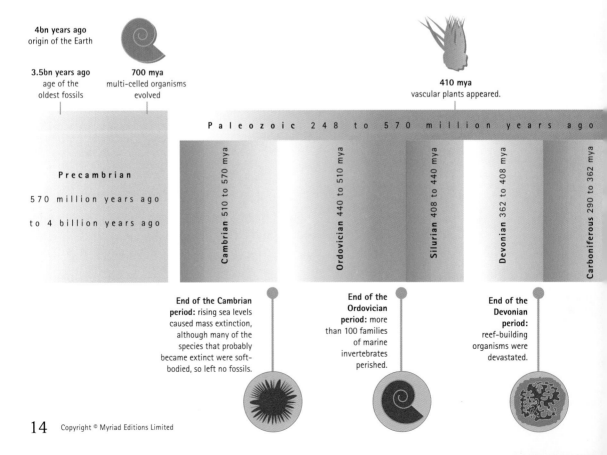

4bn years ago
origin of the Earth

3.5bn years ago
age of the oldest fossils

700 mya
multi-celled organisms evolved

410 mya
vascular plants appeared.

Paleozoic 248 to 570 million years ago

Precambrian

570 million years ago to 4 billion years ago

Cambrian 510 to 570 mya

Ordovician 440 to 510 mya

Silurian 408 to 440 mya

Devonian 362 to 408 mya

Carboniferous 290 to 362 mya

End of the Cambrian period: rising sea levels caused mass extinction, although many of the species that probably became extinct were soft-bodied, so left no fossils.

End of the Ordovician period: more than 100 families of marine invertebrates perished.

End of the Devonian period: reef-building organisms were devastated.

The present age is witness to the sixth great mass extinction. Although 1.5 million living species have been named by scientists, this is but a small fraction of the estimated 10 million to 100 million species that are thought to be alive on Earth. Most of these are likely to be destroyed by humans before they have even been identified.

TIMELINE OF MASS EXTINCTIONS
Main eras and periods

mya   millions of years ago

          mass extinction

240 mya
dinosaurs, mammals, pterosaurs (flying reptiles), amphibians (including frogs and turtles) appeared.

100,000 years ago
homo sapiens
appeared

210 mya
towards the end of the Triassic period, climate change caused an extinction of amphibians, marine reptiles and other species, setting the stage for the ascendance of dinosaurs.

190 mya
birds
appeared

130 mya
flowering plants (angiosperms) appeared

50 mya
primates
evolved

11,000 years ago
a cooling climate and hunting by humans caused extinctions among large mammals, including mammoths, huge ground sloths and saber-toothed tigers.

M e s o z o i c   65   to   248   million   years   ago   **C e n z o i c** 0 to 65 mya

Permian 248 to 290 mya

Triassic 206 to 248 mya

Jurassic 145 to 206 mya

Cretaceous 65 to 145 mya

Tertiary 2 to 65 mya

Quatenary 0 to 2 mya

End of the Permian period: between 90% and 95% of marine species disappeared, including trilobites.

End of the Cretaceous period: 85% of all species became extinct, including all dinosaurs and pterosaurs (flying reptiles).

Present: In the 20th century the rate of extinction increased to 1% each year — about 10,000 times higher than before human technological society.

DINOSAURS

This map shows the position of continents 100 million years ago. At the beginning of the dinosaur period the land mass of Pangaea formed a single supercontinent. This broke into Laurasia and Gondwanaland which, by the time of the extinction of the dinosaurs, had further separated into recognizable modern continents.

Dinosaurs (from the Greek for "terrible lizard") were reptiles that thrived all over the world for 150 million years, from around 206 million to 66 million years ago (mya). During this period dinosaurs were the dominant group of animals on land. Over 1,000 very diverse species have been identified from fossil remains in sedimentary rocks. This is probably a small fraction of the total, as the conditions required for fossils to form are rare.

Many, perhaps all, dinosaurs built nests and laid eggs. They returned to the same nesting sites year after year. Some dinosaurs were huge. Tyrannosaurus earned a fearsome reputation as predators. Pterosaurs ("pterodactyls") were flying reptiles that lived at the same time as the dinosaurs.

At various times during the reign of the dinosaurs some species became extinct. But the fossil record indicates peaks in extinction among dinosaurs at the end of the Triassic (206 mya), the end of the Jurassic (145 mya) and, finally, at the end of the Cretaceous (66 mya) periods (see *Mass Extinctions* pages 14–15).

No-one is sure what caused the final extinction of the dinosaurs. The period of the dinosaurs' demise, between the Cretaceous and Tertiary periods, is known as the "K-T boundary event". The difficulty of pinpointing events precisely from the geological record means that it is not known how long it took for the dinosaurs to die out. The most widely held contention is that a catastrophic meteorite strike threw up a colossal amount of dust and debris into the atmosphere. This would have blocked sunlight, killing plants and the animals that depended on them. Strong evidence for this theory was provided by the discovery of the rare metal iridium in rocks

corresponding in age to the K-T boundary. Meteorites have a higher concentration of iridium than is found on Earth. The site of the meteorite strike has not been definitively established, although one candidate is a crater at Chicxulub in Mexico's Yucatan Peninsula. Another possibility is that the meteorite landed in the ocean. An unresolved problem with the meteorite theory is that other groups, such as mammals and amphibians, were not severely affected.

Other hypotheses include disease and heat waves with resulting sterility, freezing cold spells, the rise of egg-eating mammals and x-rays from a supernova exploding nearby.

Not all dinosaurs died 66 million years ago. The bird Archaeopteryx, which is now also extinct, was probably descended from a small dinosaur. In fact, all birds may have originated from dinosaurs.

The Dinosaur National Monument is an area of over 300 square miles (800 sq km) in Colorado and Utah, USA. Many dinosaurs have been found in the rich fossil beds here.

The meteorite that may have been responsible for dinosaur extinction could have struck Yucatan, Mexico.

The herbivore **Argentinosaurus huinculensis** was perhaps the largest dinosaur, at over 130 feet (40m) long. It lived in what is now Argentina.

DINOSAUR FOSSILS
Location of major fossil finds
selected

position of continents
100 million years ago
estimated

Allosaurus   Argentinosaurus

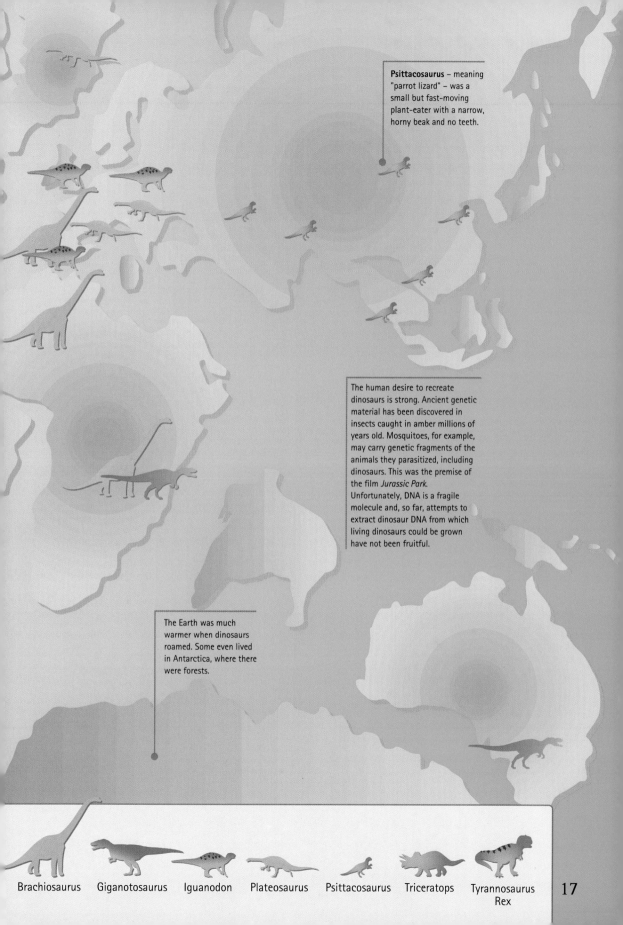

Psittacosaurus – meaning "parrot lizard" – was a small but fast-moving plant-eater with a narrow, horny beak and no teeth.

The human desire to recreate dinosaurs is strong. Ancient genetic material has been discovered in insects caught in amber millions of years old. Mosquitoes, for example, may carry genetic fragments of the animals they parasitized, including dinosaurs. This was the premise of the film *Jurassic Park*. Unfortunately, DNA is a fragile molecule and, so far, attempts to extract dinosaur DNA from which living dinosaurs could be grown have not been fruitful.

The Earth was much warmer when dinosaurs roamed. Some even lived in Antarctica, where there were forests.

Brachiosaurus   Giganotosaurus   Iguanodon   Plateosaurus   Psittacosaurus   Triceratops   Tyrannosaurus Rex

Modern humans are the last survivors of the hominid family whose many branches evolved as a result of geographic isolation, possibly brought about by climate change.

Humans are the only primates who habitually stand and move in an upright position. The oldest known hominids are the genus *Australopithecus*, which evolved from more ape-like creatures over 4 million years ago in Africa and appears not to have spread beyond that continent. Their jaws were ideally suited to feeding on fruit, nuts and berries, and they became extinct around one million years ago probably because their specialized diet became scarce as the climate became drier and savannah replaced woodland.

By the time of its demise, *Australopithecus* was not the only hominid in existence. Two and a half million years ago a larger-brained hominid developed, and evolved into a species (*Homo sapiens*) that was to dominate the planet.

Hominid skulls increased in size as the species evolved, indicating a growing mental capacity. From the size and form of different brain areas, scientists have been able to deduce how intelligence has developed: the frontal lobe indicates abstract processing and a capacity for language whilst the parietal lobe, at the top of the head, is responsible for technological and computational thinking.

It is this use of tools and technology, from clothing and housing to sophisticated farming methods, that has served as a buffer between *Homo sapiens* and the changing environment. Alterations in the population gene pool that lead eventually to new species developing have not been identified in humans for the last 250,000 years.

About two and a half million years ago hominids began fashioning bladed tools by chipping rocks. The same ability for technological and computational thinking now presents opportunities for genetic manipulation and artificial body-parts – a development that may lead to the most rapid period of hominid evolution yet witnessed.

Homo neanderthalensis lived in Southern Europe 100,000 years ago. Up until about 30,000 years ago, they co-existed with modern humans. Their demise may have been due to competition for resources with humans or it is possible they met a more violent end. Alternative theories suggest that Neanderthals were adapted to cold conditions and disappeared as the climate grew warmer. Although some scientists argue that Neanderthals gave rise to modern humans, most agree that they are not our direct ancestors.

Hominids are human-like primates, descended from the genus **Homo**. Bones of *Homo erectus* have been discovered across South and Southeast Asia. They became extinct about 150,000 years ago – before the appearance of *Homo sapiens* around 120,000 years ago.

FOSSIL FINDS IN AFRICA

- area where fossils have been found
- **A** Australopithecus
- **H** Homo

H erectus

H erectus

A bahrelghazali

A afarensis

A anamensis
A afarensis
A boisei
H erectus
H habilis
H rudolfensis

A africanus
A robustus
H habilis

Most fossil finds are just fragments, such as a tooth or a piece of skull. **"Lucy"** is special because almost half of her skeleton was recovered and DNA testing showed that she lived 3.2 million years ago.

Lucy was discovered in the Hatar Valley in Ethiopia by Donald Johanson in 1974, and named after the Beatles' song, "Lucy in the Sky with Diamonds" (remade by Elton John that year). Lucy was probably around 25 years old when she died. She would have stood about 3 feet 6 inches (1.10 meters) tall, although other *Australopithecus afarensis* from this area were up to 5 feet 8 inches (1.70 meters) tall.

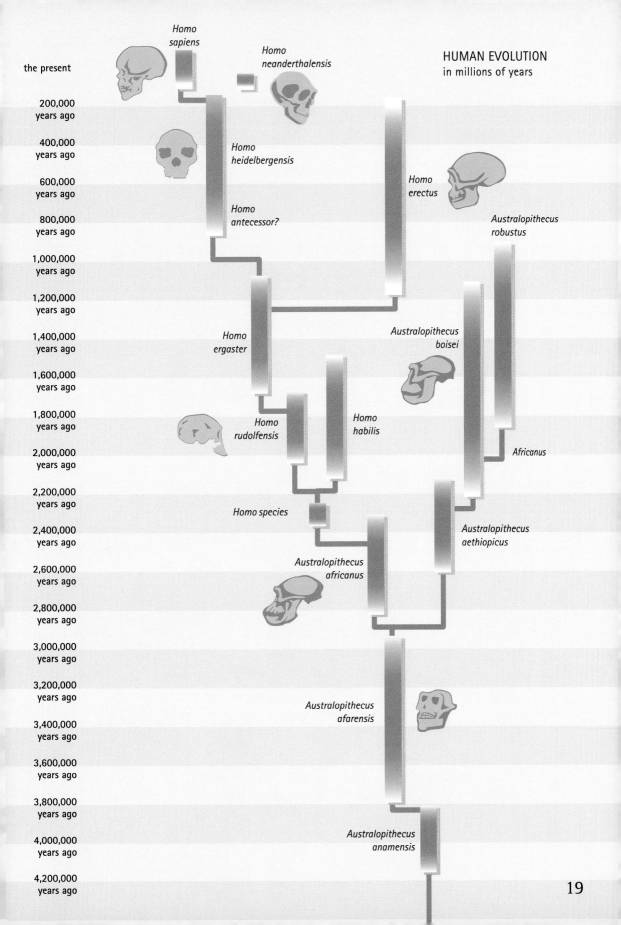

ECOSYSTEMS

"Try to imagine the Earth without ecosystems...
Each ecosystem represents a solution to a particular
challenge to life, worked out over millennia...
Stripped of its ecosystems, Earth would resemble
the stark, lifeless images beamed back from Mars..."

— *World Resources 2000–2001*

The area bounded by the Tropic of Cancer (23.5°N) and the Tropic of Capricorn (23.5°S) is known as "the tropics". Tropical rainforest, mainly comprised of evergreen trees, thrives in areas of high rainfall. Deciduous trees, which shed their leaves in the dry season, tend to grow in areas where there is a seasonal drought. In dry areas that are prone to fire, and where soils are particularly poor, trees grow sparsely, forming "woody savanna".

Tropical forests bind the soil, helping to prevent erosion and retain the few nutrients present. They also absorb carbon dioxide from the atmosphere, exchanging it for oxygen. Tropical forests cover only 6 percent of the Earth's land area but probably contain over half the world's species, most of which have yet to be identified.

Fire, often caused by lightning, is part of the natural cycle of regeneration in tropical forests. Fire destroys the forest canopy, enabling light to reach the ground, and saplings and herbs to grow. In most cases, however, forest fires are caused by humans. In some cases they are deliberately lit in order to clear forests for agriculture. In others, they are started inadvertently, perhaps by discarded cigarettes or sparks from machinery.

Clearing by slashing and burning techniques, and more recently by machines, may completely destroy the remaining major areas of tropical forests. Many of the tropical forests are in poor countries whose priorities are to clear land for agriculture. Attempts by wealthier countries to encourage development often lead to tropical forests being exploited for timber.

Once the forest is gone, the land is prone to erosion and flooding. Nutrients in the soil are rapidly leached and after a few years farming and ranching become untenable. Where the original forest cover is substantial, as in the Amazon, it has a major influence on climate. Loss of trees reduces local rainfall and may even disrupt the global climate. Sustainable exploitation of tropical forests, including selective logging and harvesting of products such as fruit and rubber, can provide a higher long-term income than more destructive practices.

PROTECTED TROPICAL FOREST
Percentage of tropical forest protected *1996*

- 50% or more
- 30.0% – 49.9%
- 10.0% – 29.9%
- 5.0% – 9.9%
- 0.1% – 4.9%
- 0% or no data
- no tropical forest

The **mahogany tree** is prized worldwide for its dark timber, and about 40% of mahogany logged in Brazil is exported to make furniture. The trees grow slowly, at low density, and the mahogany is already extinct in Honduras and Colombia.

UNITED STATES OF AMERICA

MEXICO

CUBA
DOMINICAN REPUBLIC
BELIZE JAMAICA HAITI
GUATEMALA HONDURAS
EL SALVADOR
NICARAGUA
COSTA RICA
TRINIDAD & TOBAGO
PANAMA
VENEZUELA GUYANA
SURINAME
COLOMBIA
ECUADOR

SENEGAL
GAMBIA
GUINEA-BISSAU
GUINEA
SIERRA LEONE
LIBERIA

BRAZIL

PERU

BOLIVIA

PARAGUAY

ARGENTINA

TROPICAL FOREST BY REGION
Protected tropical forest as percentage of tropical forest in the region *1996*

tropical forest area in thousand hectares

percentage protected

Asia
16.4%

210,720

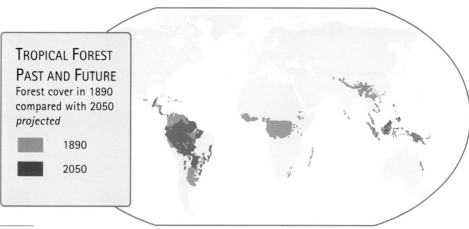

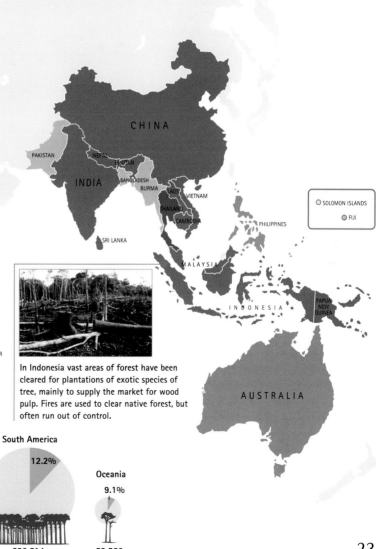

Tropical forests in the **Congo basin** are being degraded at a rate that may see them disappear by 2050, as rapid population growth and a desperate need to repay international debt drives indiscriminate logging.

○ SOLOMON ISLANDS
◉ FIJI

In Indonesia vast areas of forest have been cleared for plantations of exotic species of tree, mainly to supply the market for wood pulp. Fires are used to clear native forest, but often run out of control.

Sub-Saharan Africa
9.1%

Central America and Caribbean
12%

South America
12.2%

Oceania
9.1%

448,063

70,812

620,514

53,560

TEMPERATE FORESTS

Temperate regions lie to the north and south of the tropics (23.5° latitude). Deciduous temperate trees that shed their leaves each winter form much of the forest in the higher latitudes. In the lower latitudes "boreal" forests of conifers cover the largest area of any forest type in the world. Conifers also dominate forests at higher altitudes in most temperate latitudes and in places where soils are poor.

Temperate forests have been cleared for agriculture and felled for timber for thousands of years. In the late 20th century this trend slowed as populations in temperate regions stabilized and resources other than timber were used for fuel and building materials. In the 1990s the area of temperate forest cover worldwide rose. However, the ecological quality of many forests has continued to decline as plantations replaced "old growth" forests and the frequency of fires has risen. Fires started by people consume an average of one percent of the existing Mediterranean forest every year.

Inappropriate planting of trees to act as "carbon sinks", a measure to counteract global warming, can actually reduce biodiversity. Most plantations are comprised of a few or even a single tree species such as eucalyptus and pine that may be alien to that habitat. Plantations do, however, make an indirect contribution to conservation by relieving the need to log "old growth" forests.

When forests become fragmented the plants and animals in each forest fragment can be isolated from adjacent forests and local extinction may result. It also becomes more difficult for species to migrate in response to climate change.

Pollution has also damaged temperate forests. The burning of fossil fuels releases sulfur and nitrogen into the atmosphere. Transported by the wind this can fall to earth as dry deposits or combine with water to form "acid rain". Polluting gases are also converted by sunlight into ozone, which interferes with the biological functioning of plants. Forests hundreds of miles from industrial centers are affected, in particular those in the northeast of North America, in East Asia and in northeastern Europe and Scandinavia.

TEMPERATE FOREST BY REGION

Protected temperate forest as percentage of temperate forest in the region *1996*

temperate forest area in thousand hectares

percentage protected

Asia
5.3%
132,065

North America
8.9%
683,700

South America
15.8%
39,178

Europe
3%
991,346

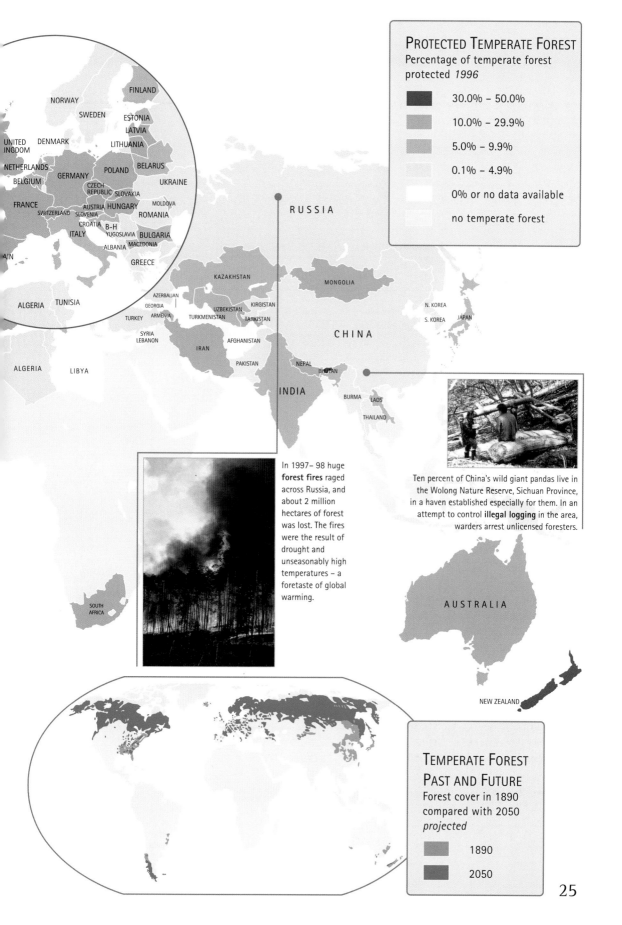

FINLAND
NORWAY
SWEDEN
ESTONIA
LATVIA
UNITED KINGDOM
DENMARK
LITHUANIA
NETHERLANDS
BELARUS
GERMANY
POLAND
BELGIUM
CZECH REPUBLIC
UKRAINE
SLOVAKIA
FRANCE
AUSTRIA
HUNGARY
MOLDOVA
SWITZERLAND
SLOVENIA
ROMANIA
CROATIA
ITALY
B-H
YUGOSLAVIA
BULGARIA
ALBANIA
MACEDONIA
GREECE

RUSSIA

ALGERIA
TUNISIA

KAZAKHSTAN
MONGOLIA

AZERBAIJAN
GEORGIA
UZBEKISTAN
KIRGISTAN
N. KOREA
TURKEY
ARMENIA
TURKMENISTAN
TAJIKISTAN
S. KOREA
JAPAN
SYRIA
LEBANON
CHINA
IRAN
AFGHANISTAN
ALGERIA
LIBYA
PAKISTAN
NEPAL
BHUTAN
INDIA
BURMA
LAOS
THAILAND

In 1997– 98 huge **forest fires** raged across Russia, and about 2 million hectares of forest was lost. The fires were the result of drought and unseasonably high temperatures – a foretaste of global warming.

Ten percent of China's wild giant pandas live in the Wolong Nature Reserve, Sichuan Province, in a haven established especially for them. In an attempt to control **illegal logging** in the area, warders arrest unlicensed foresters.

SOUTH AFRICA

AUSTRALIA

NEW ZEALAND

TEMPERATE FOREST PAST AND FUTURE
Forest cover in 1890 compared with 2050 *projected*

- 1890
- 2050

25

GRASSLANDS

Grassland covers more of the Earth's surface than any other type of terrain. Estimates range from 31 percent to 43 percent, depending on the definition of "grassland", which can include savanna, prairie, scrub, high-altitude plains and Arctic tundra. More than 70 percent of some African countries are covered in grassland, and grassland makes up more than half the terrain in around 40 countries. One of the defining characteristics of grassland is that its vegetation is prevented from turning into forest by fire, grazing, lack of water or by freezing temperatures.

Grasslands support a wide range of wild animals, in particular birds. As well as providing year-round habitat for endemic bird species, grasslands also provide temporary refuge and breeding sites for migrating birds. They are therefore of vital importance, and their degradation in North America has resulted in a declining bird population since the mid-1960s.

Grasslands also provide grazing for domestic animals. In some areas of the world they have supported nomadic herds of sheep, goats and cattle for thousands of years. With growing human populations rearing ever more livestock, however, grasslands are at risk from over-grazing, which leads to soil erosion.

One of the major threats to grassland ecosystems is fragmentation by development, including roads. Breaking grassland up into small patches reduces its capacity to maintain biological diversity – it becomes degraded. This is what is happening in the Great Plains of the USA, where criss-crossing roads have fragmented 70 percent of the area into patches smaller than 386 square miles (1,000 square kilometres).

Much of the watershed areas of many of the world's largest rivers are comprised of grassland. Here it performs the vital function of absorbing rainfall into underground aquifers that in turn feed into the river systems. Grasslands also absorb carbon emissions, holding an estimated 33 percent of carbon stored in terrestrial ecosystems, most of which is to be found in the soil.

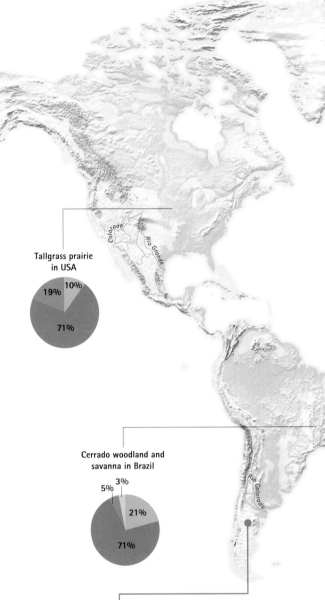

Tallgrass prairie in USA
10%
19%
71%

Cerrado woodland and savanna in Brazil
3%
5%
21%
71%

The dry **Patagonian steppe** in Argentina hosts abundant wildlife, including the endemic wild llama, the "guanaco". Human settlement is limited to "estancias" (ranches) and a few small towns. Its aridity leaves the Patagonian steppe vulnerable to overgrazing by sheep and goats, which are turning some areas into desert. Pumas are hunted, often illegally, because they prey on livestock.

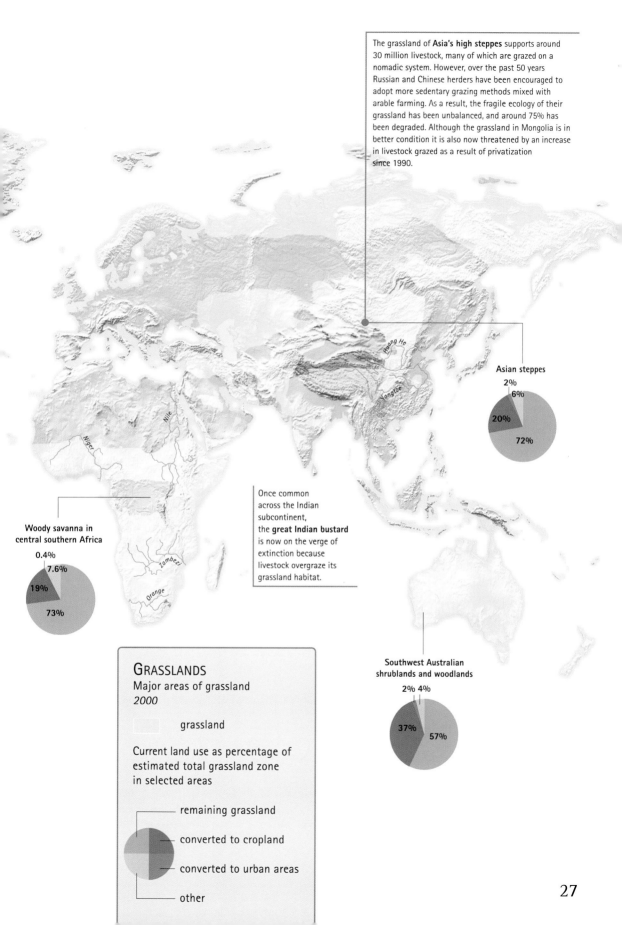

The grassland of **Asia's high steppes** supports around 30 million livestock, many of which are grazed on a nomadic system. However, over the past 50 years Russian and Chinese herders have been encouraged to adopt more sedentary grazing methods mixed with arable farming. As a result, the fragile ecology of their grassland has been unbalanced, and around 75% has been degraded. Although the grassland in Mongolia is in better condition it is also now threatened by an increase in livestock grazed as a result of privatization since 1990.

Asian steppes
2%
6%
20%
72%

Once common across the Indian subcontinent, the **great Indian bustard** is now on the verge of extinction because livestock overgraze its grassland habitat.

Woody savanna in central southern Africa
0.4%
7.6%
19%
73%

Southwest Australian shrublands and woodlands
2% 4%
37%
57%

GRASSLANDS
Major areas of grassland
2000

◻ grassland

Current land use as percentage of estimated total grassland zone in selected areas

— remaining grassland

— converted to cropland

— converted to urban areas

— other

27

WETLANDS

Wetlands are among the world's richest and most productive ecosystems. They include swamps, marshes, and mangroves and cover around 2 million square miles (over 5 million sq km) worldwide. Salt marshes, especially, support a large number of invertebrates which, in turn, are preyed upon by diverse species of birds. Coral reefs (see pages 32–33) are considered to be "marine wetlands".

Wetlands occur on poorly drained land. Where there are few nutrients, organic matter decays very slowly and peat accumulates beneath the living plants to create bogs. At northern latitudes, low temperatures make the rate of decay even slower, and mosses such as *sphagnum* dominate the flora. In wetland areas where the soil has more nutrients, both inland and at the mouths of great rivers such as the Mississippi and the Nile, grass grows to form marshes. Inter-tidal salt marshes occur around river deltas and elsewhere along temperate coasts.

Many wetland areas have been lost in Europe, and in the USA around half of all wetlands have been lost to urban development. Inter-tidal salt marshes have been developed for ports, marinas and residential construction. In Asia and Africa wetlands are being polluted by shrimp farming.

Agriculture is the principal cause of wetland loss worldwide, with wetlands being drained to provide land for crops. The damming of rivers for hydro-electric power can disrupt the ecology of wetlands downstream. Wetlands provide excellent breeding grounds for mosquitoes, and many have been drained in an attempt to control malaria.

The Convention on Wetlands was signed in Ramsar, Iran in 1971. By 2001, signatory nations had designated over 81 million hectares of the largest, most biodiverse and unique wetlands in 1,073 sites for inclusion in the Ramsar List of Wetlands of International Importance. They undertake to practice "wise use" of those wetlands, and to sustain their biodiversity.

By 1870 North American smooth cord-grass had spread to western Europe, probably in ships. It interbred with the native short cord-grass to produce the vigorous **common cord-grass**. This hybrid colonized extensive mud flats, preventing large wintering populations of waders and wildfowl from feeding and roosting. Pesticides and uprooting have been used to eliminate common cord-grass from nature reserves.

COASTAL DEVELOPMENT
Level of threat from development *1995*

—— high

—— moderate

—— low

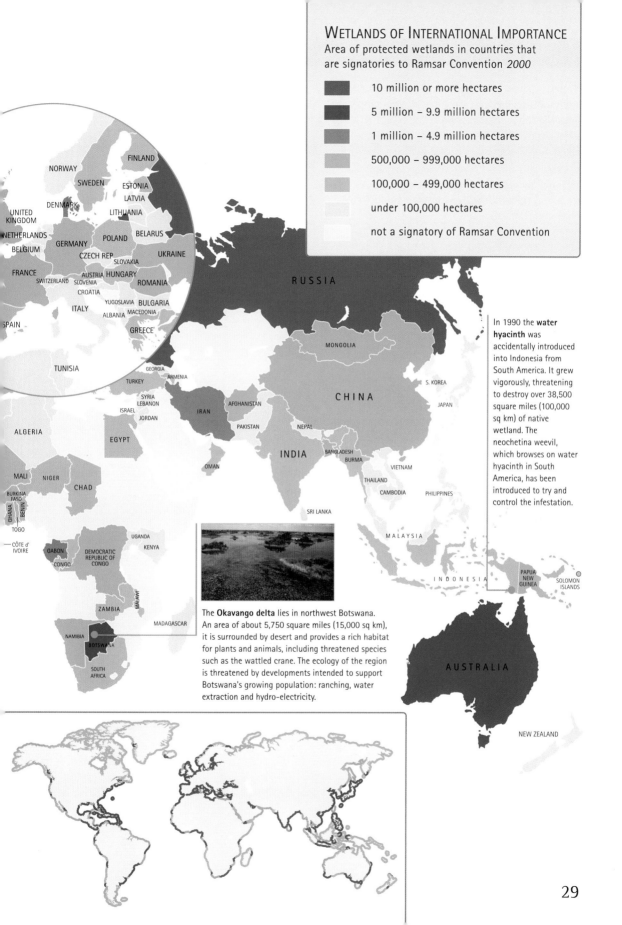

WETLANDS OF INTERNATIONAL IMPORTANCE
Area of protected wetlands in countries that are signatories to Ramsar Convention 2000

- 10 million or more hectares
- 5 million – 9.9 million hectares
- 1 million – 4.9 million hectares
- 500,000 – 999,000 hectares
- 100,000 – 499,000 hectares
- under 100,000 hectares
- not a signatory of Ramsar Convention

In 1990 the **water hyacinth** was accidentally introduced into Indonesia from South America. It grew vigorously, threatening to destroy over 38,500 square miles (100,000 sq km) of native wetland. The neochetina weevil, which browses on water hyacinth in South America, has been introduced to try and control the infestation.

The **Okavango delta** lies in northwest Botswana. An area of about 5,750 square miles (15,000 sq km), it is surrounded by desert and provides a rich habitat for plants and animals, including threatened species such as the wattled crane. The ecology of the region is threatened by developments intended to support Botswana's growing population: ranching, water extraction and hydro-electricity.

MANGROVES

Mangroves are marine tidal forests. They are found in rainy tropical countries, usually around the mouths of large rivers and in sheltered bays. They help to stabilize the banks of estuaries and reduce erosion, and support many plants and animals, including lichens, epiphytes, and bacteria. Mangrove forests also provide vital nursery areas and feeding sites for many species of fish, crustacea, and shellfish, as well as nesting sites for birds.

Mangrove forests are found in some 70 countries and cover about 70,000 square miles (181,000 sq km) worldwide, but this represents only about half of their original extent; they once covered three-quarters of the coastlines of tropical and sub-tropical countries.

Of the mangrove forest remaining today, 50 percent is considered to be degraded by human development. Many mangroves have been lost to the timber industry, and to commercial development such as that at Tampa Bay in Florida, USA (see right). Elsewhere, shrimp farms are expanding to satisfy a growing world demand, but slack regulation of the industry by national governments, and the headlong rush of aquaculture development, has led to the destruction of mangrove forests. In South East Asia, especially, mangroves are being severely depleted, with possibly only 30 percent of the original mangrove forest remaining across the region.

Mangrove deforestation affects not only the species that rely on them for food and shelter but also the land itself: the loss of these forests causes erosion and land subsidence and permits salt water to penetrate coastal soils, jeopardizing their use for agriculture and threatening clean water supplies. Destruction of mangroves also releases carbon dioxide into the atmosphere, contributing to climate change and affecting nearby fisheries.

FLORIDA MANGROVES

- ▮ mangroves
- — boundary of National Park

Tampa
Florida
Lake Worth
Miami
Everglades National Park World Heritage Site
Biscayne Bay National Park
Florida Keys

Florida has an estimated 765 square miles (2,000 sq km) of mangrove forests, comprising three different species: the red, black and white mangrove. During the 20th century large swathes were destroyed as the area was developed, including 44% in Tampa Bay, and 87% of those around Lake Worth. Even the conservation measures adopted in the Everglades National Park are not enough to protect it from water pollution. Florida's wading bird population, depending on mangroves for their nesting areas, have declined to around ten percent of their original level.

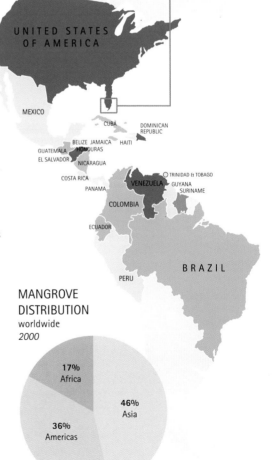

UNITED STATES OF AMERICA

MEXICO

CUBA
DOMINICAN REPUBLIC
BELIZE JAMAICA HAITI
GUATEMALA HONDURAS
EL SALVADOR
NICARAGUA
COSTA RICA
TRINIDAD & TOBAGO
PANAMA
VENEZUELA GUYANA
SURINAME
COLOMBIA
ECUADOR
PERU
BRAZIL

SENEGAL —
GAMBIA —
GUINEA-BISSAU —
GUINEA —
SIERRA LEONE —
CÔTE d'IVOIRE —

MANGROVE DISTRIBUTION
worldwide
2000

- 17% Africa
- 46% Asia
- 36% Americas

The total annual value of ecosystem services provided by tidal marshes and mangroves worldwide is estimated at US $1.6 trillion.

MANGROVE LOSS IN THAILAND
Total area of mangroves
square miles (square kilometres)
1961–1993

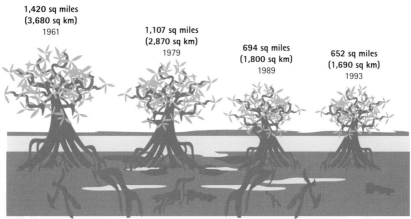

**1,420 sq miles
(3,680 sq km)**
1961

**1,107 sq miles
(2,870 sq km)**
1979

**694 sq miles
(1,800 sq km)**
1989

**652 sq miles
(1,690 sq km)**
1993

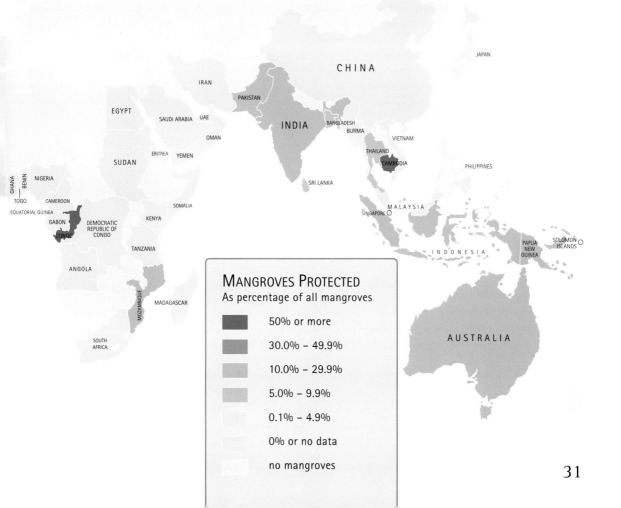

MANGROVES PROTECTED
As percentage of all mangroves

- 50% or more
- 30.0% – 49.9%
- 10.0% – 29.9%
- 5.0% – 9.9%
- 0.1% – 4.9%
- 0% or no data
- no mangroves

31

CORAL REEFS

Coral consists of thousands of invertebrate marine animals – known as "polyps" – with a hollow, cylindrical structure and a skeleton containing calcium carbonate. The lower end of the coral is attached to a rock or another polyp. At the free end is a mouth, surrounded by tentacles that can be extended to paralyze prey.

Coral reefs form in shallow ocean areas. Initial polyps divide into daughter polyps, which in turn divide to form colonies that can grow up to several yards wide. Corals are found in the waters of over 100 countries. They grow profusely in warm, well-circulating calm waters and cover an estimated 231,600 square miles (600,000 sq km) worldwide. Home to a vast number of different species, coral reefs are second only to rainforests in species richness.

Sick coral provides an early warning that entire ecosystems are in danger. Since the 1980s, dozens of new infections, including white band and yellow pox, have attacked corals. Few of these ailments have a known cause, but human development of coastal zones is a likely factor.

Increases in sea temperature and levels, and alterations to ocean currents, can cause individual polyps to "bleach". With increasing climate changes, corals may not fully recover.

Forest clearance and intensive agriculture can wash soil into rivers and out to sea, silting up reefs. Sunlight is vital for coral growth but murky water prevents it reaching the reefs. The mangroves that protect reefs from terrestrial sediments are themselves under threat (see *Mangroves* pages 30-31). When poorly treated sewage and fertilizer run-off flows over reefs, algae multiply in the nutrient-rich water, cover and choke the coral polyps.

Illegal fishing methods, such as the use of cyanide and explosives to stun fish, also damages coral. Over-fishing also affects the ecological balance of a reef, which can become overgrown with algae if grazing fish are removed.

The loss of coral reefs is likely to reduce the fish catch of many tropical developing countries, around 25 percent of which comes from reef environments. Where reefs may have acted as barriers against erosion, their destruction may also allow the sea to encroach on coastal regions.

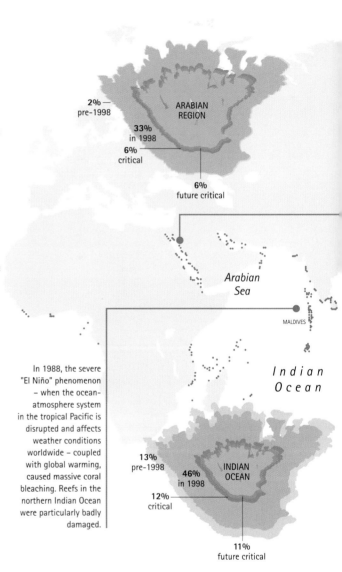

2% — pre-1998

33% in 1998

6% critical

ARABIAN REGION

6% future critical

CAPE VERDE

Arabian Sea

MALDIVES

In 1988, the severe "El Niño" phenomenon – when the ocean-atmosphere system in the tropical Pacific is disrupted and affects weather conditions worldwide – coupled with global warming, caused massive coral bleaching. Reefs in the northern Indian Ocean were particularly badly damaged.

I n d i a n   O c e a n

13% pre-1998

46% in 1998

INDIAN OCEAN

12% critical

11% future critical

Two-thirds of all damage to coral in the Red Sea is caused by tourism, with tourists buying or taking coral, and inexperienced divers colliding with reefs. Carefully managed tourism could save reefs by developing the marine parks which act as breeding grounds for fish. However, although over 350 protected areas include coral reefs, these are often in countries without adequate resources to enforce the necessary controls.

Two-thirds of all damage to coral in the Red Sea is caused by tourism, with tourists buying or taking coral, and inexperienced divers colliding with reefs.

During the 1980s white band disease, caused by a bacterium related to cholera, nearly wiped out *Acropora* corals across the Caribbean, where they had dominated coral communities for at least 4,000 years.

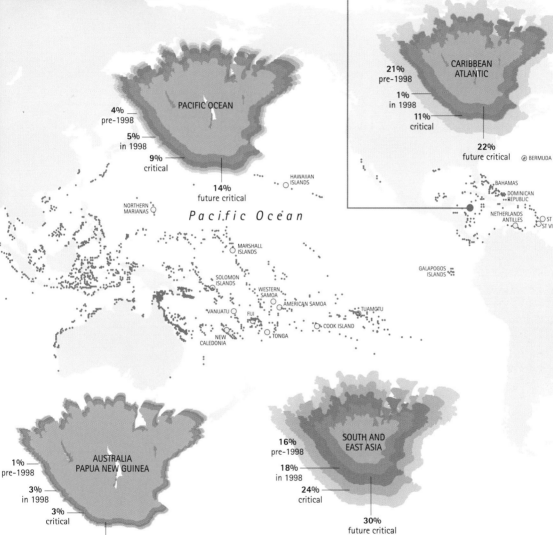

CARIBBEAN ATLANTIC

21% pre-1998

1% in 1998

11% critical

22% future critical

⊚ BERMUDA

BAHAMAS

DOMINICAN REPUBLIC

NETHERLANDS ANTILLES

ST LUCIA
ST VINCENT

GALAPOGOS ISLANDS

PACIFIC OCEAN

4% pre-1998

5% in 1998

9% critical

14% future critical

HAWAIIAN ISLANDS

Pacific Ocean

NORTHERN MARIANAS

MARSHALL ISLANDS

SOLOMON ISLANDS

WESTERN SAMOA

AMERICAN SAMOA

VANUATU

FIJI

TUAMOTU

COOK ISLAND

NEW CALEDONIA

TONGA

AUSTRALIA PAPUA NEW GUINEA

1% pre-1998

3% in 1998

3% critical

6% future critical

SOUTH AND EAST ASIA

16% pre-1998

18% in 1998

24% critical

30% future critical

THE STATE OF CORAL

 coral reefs

Coral reef destroyed
percentage of total given

 before 1998

 in 1998

Coral reef expected to be destroyed in future
percentage of total given

 1998 – 2008 *projected*

 2008 – 2028 *projected*

Coral expected to remain healthy

 2028 *projected*

FRAGILE REGIONS

"There are no passengers on spaceship earth.
We are all crew."

– Marshall McLuhan

The Arctic presents some of the harshest conditions on the planet but is home to unique and fragile communities. Plants that are dormant for most of the year blossom during the brief Arctic summer. Vast numbers of birds, including over a hundred species of waterfowl and waders, breed and then migrate all over the world. Animals, such as polar bears, arctic foxes and seals, breed and then remain to over-winter.

Polar bears used to be widely hunted for their skins and meat. By 1970 their numbers had fallen below 10,000. In 1973 Canada, Denmark (which governs Greenland), Norway, the USA, and what was the USSR signed the International Agreement on Conservation of Polar Bears and Their Habitat. The treaty protects the polar bears' feeding and breeding grounds and their migration routes. It also bans the capture of polar bears, except by scientists working to preserve the species, and by the Inuit, who are allowed to hunt only a certain number each year, and are banned from doing so when female bears are pregnant or with their cubs.

The countries have established reserves where polar bears are completely protected. The international agreement also states that all five nations must ban polar-bear hunting from aircraft and large motorized boats, conduct and co-ordinate management and research efforts, and exchange research results and data. Since 1973 the polar bear population has risen again to between 20,000 and 40,000.

Hunting is not the only threat to Arctic wildlife. In recent years warmer Atlantic Ocean water has penetrated the Arctic Ocean basin. Arctic ice cover and salinity have declined as the ice-cap has melted. Permafrost soils in Alaska, Canada and Russia are thawing. Buildings, roads, oil pipelines and other structures built on the frozen hard soils suffer damage as a result. Whether these changes are part of a short-term natural cycle or a manifestation of global warming is the subject of intense scientific study. Shrinking sea-ice in the Arctic will cause reductions in ice algae, which live beneath the ice and form the base of the Arctic food chain. This will affect fish, seals, whales and polar bears. Polar bears are already suffering from the loss of their hunting grounds on ice-shelves. Global warming will also cause forests to move north, replacing the Arctic tundra, affecting birds, such as the critically endangered red-breasted goose (see below), that breed in the tundra.

Persistent organic pollutants (POPs) are produced by industries all over the world. They are wafted to the Arctic by wind and sea, and also by migrating animals. Arctic wildlife is exposed to DDT (a pesticide), PCBs (from electronic equipment), and dioxins (from plastics). POPs are not excreted by animals, but accumulate in their fatty tissue. Those highest up the food chain, such as seals and polar bears, are most severely exposed. These chemicals can affect fertility and damage the immune system. Heavy metals, including mercury, arsenic, and lead are also carried to the Arctic.

Collaboration between polar nations to address these wider problems is co-ordinated by the Arctic Council. The deeper causes of many of the problems facing the Arctic, such as global warming and industrial pollution, lie much further to the south, in the energy-heavy rich industrialized nations, and can only be tackled there.

RED-BREASTED GOOSE
Population in Europe
1992 – 1994
numbers

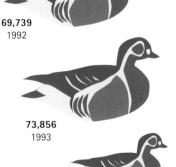

69,739
1992

73,856
1993

37,355
1994

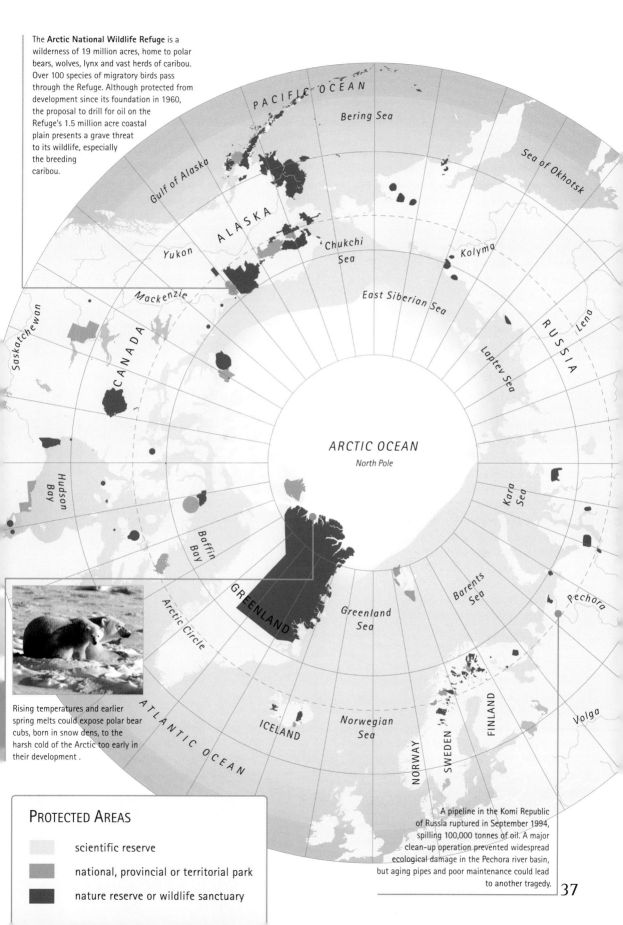

The **Arctic National Wildlife Refuge** is a wilderness of 19 million acres, home to polar bears, wolves, lynx and vast herds of caribou. Over 100 species of migratory birds pass through the Refuge. Although protected from development since its foundation in 1960, the proposal to drill for oil on the Refuge's 1.5 million acre coastal plain presents a grave threat to its wildlife, especially the breeding caribou.

PACIFIC OCEAN

Bering Sea

Sea of Okhotsk

Gulf of Alaska

ALASKA

Yukon

Chukchi Sea

Kolyma

Mackenzie

East Siberian Sea

RUSSIA

Lena

Saskatchewan

CANADA

Laptev Sea

ARCTIC OCEAN
North Pole

Kara Sea

Hudson Bay

Baffin Bay

GREENLAND

Barents Sea

Pechora

Arctic Circle

Greenland Sea

Rising temperatures and earlier spring melts could expose polar bear cubs, born in snow dens, to the harsh cold of the Arctic too early in their development .

ATLANTIC OCEAN

ICELAND

Norwegian Sea

NORWAY

SWEDEN

FINLAND

Volga

PROTECTED AREAS

scientific reserve

national, provincial or territorial park

nature reserve or wildlife sanctuary

A pipeline in the Komi Republic of Russia ruptured in September 1994, spilling 100,000 tonnes of oil. A major clean-up operation prevented widespread ecological damage in the Pechora river basin, but aging pipes and poor maintenance could lead to another tragedy.

37

The Antarctic is a continent larger than Europe, measuring 5.4 million square miles (14 million sq kms). Temperatures rarely rise above freezing, and most of the land is covered in ice. Glaciers flow from the interior into the ocean, creating enormous, half-mile thick ice-shelves.

Life flourishes despite these severe conditions. Mosses and lichens grow around the coasts and on the islands, and tiny worms and other invertebrates live on the land. In Antarctic waters there is a rich diversity of life forms. Microscopic plankton provide food for small crustaceans called krill, which in turn are eaten by fish, seabirds, and mammals. But global warming poses a threat to life in the Anartic. Its phytoplankton and fish are vulnerable to even small rises in temperature. Warmer sea temperatures would also stunt the growth of krill, leading to a shortage of food for young animals and seabirds.

Commercial krill fishing began in the 1970s, but fears that krill might be over-exploited led to a Convention on the Conservation of Antarctic Marine Living Resources in 1981. The Convention restricts krill fishing to no more than 400,000 tonnes annually. Russia and, to a lesser extent, Japan are the major krill-fishing countries.

Although the use of drift-nets, which kills many birds and dolphins, has been reduced, seabirds such as the giant wandering albatross are still becoming ensnared in long fishing lines.

Antarctic ice-fish and fin-fish have been exploited and their numbers have dwindled. Illegal fishing boats in the Antarctic may be responsible for five times more fish being landed than the reported 120,000 tonnes, and are certainly breaking the ban on whaling within the Southern Ocean Sanctuary (see opposite).

Seven countries (Argentina, Australia, Chile, France, New Zealand, Norway, and the UK) have laid claim to parts of the Antarctic, although their sovereignty is not recognized by most other nations. The Antarctic Treaty, which came into force in 1961, promotes scientific co-operation between nations on the continent and islands in the polar region. It prohibits military activity, such as weapons testing, and waste dumping. Countries participating in the Antarctic Treaty system designate Specially Protected Areas in which access is restricted in order to leave important wildlife features undisturbed.

Scientists working in the Antarctic were the first to identify a hole in the stratospheric ozone layer, caused largely by the industrial emission of chlorofluorocarbons (CFCs). The resulting increase in ultraviolet radiation is damaging the DNA of phytoplankton, fish, and krill.

Fortunately for Antarctic wildlife, there are insufficient minerals to make mining commercially viable. The human population on the continent is therefore limited mainly to scientists, and largely restricted to the summer months. Until the mid-1980s the various national scientific bases located across the continent were responsible for high levels of local contamination (waste products, oil and rubbish). More recently, the scientific community has realized the importance of maintaining the Antarctic, in its pristine state, as far as possible.

The terrain serves as a living laboratory. The lichens growing on the rocks of the cold, dry valleys of Victoria Land, for example, give vital clues to life in severe conditions, such as those present millions of years ago on Mars, as well as the relationship between populations of natural predators and their prey which – among other things – may lead to better management of fisheries worldwide.

Threatened Antarctic species include the **Rockhopper** and **Macaroni penguins**, several types of albatross – Amsterdam, Wandering, Indian Yellow-nosed, Grey-headed, Salvin's and Sooty –the Southern Giant and White-chinned petrels, the Eaton's Pintail duck, and the Blue and Fin whales.

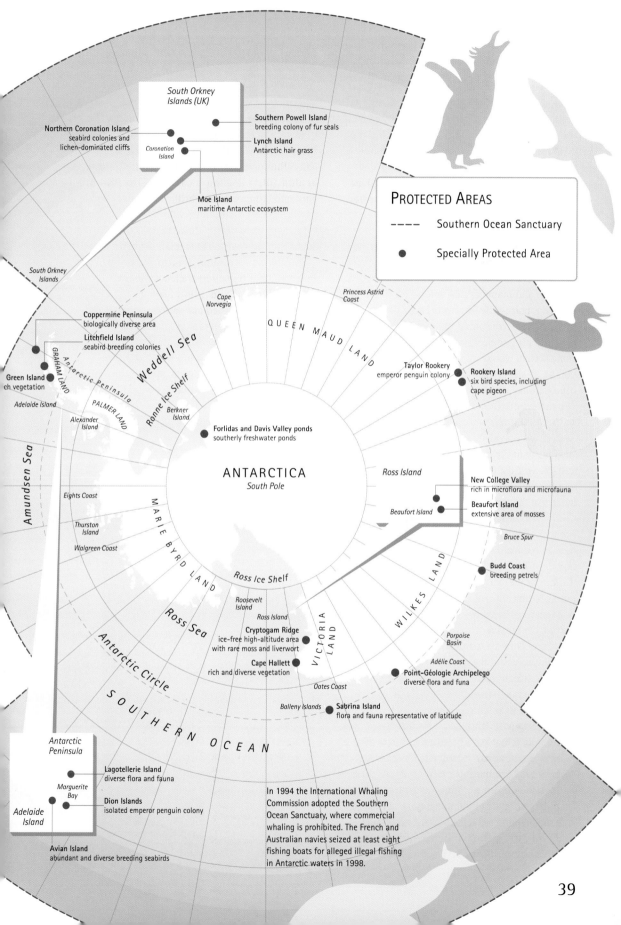

South Orkney
Islands (UK)

Northern Coronation Island
seabird colonies and
lichen-dominated cliffs

Coronation Island

Southern Powell Island
breeding colony of fur seals

Lynch Island
Antarctic hair grass

Moe Island
maritime Antarctic ecosystem

PROTECTED AREAS

- - - - Southern Ocean Sanctuary

● Specially Protected Area

South Orkney Islands

Cape Norvegia

Princess Astrid Coast

QUEEN MAUD LAND

Coppermine Peninsula
biologically diverse area

Litchfield Island
seabird breeding colonies

Weddell Sea

Taylor Rookery
emperor penguin colony

Rookery Island
six bird species, including
cape pigeon

Green Island
ch vegetation

GRAHAM LAND

Antarctic Peninsula

Ronne Ice Shelf

Adelaide Island

PALMER LAND

Alexander Island

Berkner Island

Forlidas and Davis Valley ponds
southerly freshwater ponds

Amundsen Sea

Eights Coast

MARIE BYRD LAND

Thurston Island

Walgreen Coast

ANTARCTICA
South Pole

Ross Island

New College Valley
rich in microflora and microfauna

Beaufort Island
extensive area of mosses

Beaufort Island

Bruce Spur

Budd Coast
breeding petrels

WILKES LAND

Ross Ice Shelf

Ross Sea

Roosevelt Island

Ross Island

Cryptogam Ridge
ice-free high-altitude area
with rare moss and liverwort

Cape Hallett
rich and diverse vegetation

VICTORIA LAND

Oates Coast

Porpoise Basin

Adélie Coast

Point-Géologie Archipelego
diverse flora and funa

Antarctic Circle

SOUTHERN OCEAN

Balleny Islands

Sabrina Island
flora and fauna representative of latitude

Antarctic
Peninsula

Lagotellerie Island
diverse flora and fauna

Marguerite Bay

Dion Islands
isolated emperor penguin colony

Adelaide Island

Avian Island
abundant and diverse breeding seabirds

In 1994 the International Whaling
Commission adopted the Southern
Ocean Sanctuary, where commercial
whaling is prohibited. The French and
Australian navies seized at least eight
fishing boats for alleged illegal fishing
in Antarctic waters in 1998.

AUSTRALIA

At 3 million square miles (8 million sq km), Australia is the world's smallest continent. Yet its terrain is incredibly diverse, ranging from its central deserts to the rainforests of Queensland and Tasmania. The unique plant and animal life found in Australia is a reflection of its geographical isolation. Marsupials, or pouched mammals, such as the kangaroo or koala, have evolved into species as diverse as foetal mammals elsewhere in the world.

In an attempt to preserve Australia's rich biodiversity Unesco has designated a number of World Heritage Sites. Although some of these are recognized for their fossils, most have been awarded their special status because of the need to protect unique natural habitats.

Australia's flora and fauna are sensitive both to climate changes and to those brought about by humans. Some 34 species of animal are known to have become extinct in the past 30,000 years. The extinctions prior to the arrival of European settlers in the late 18th century were largely caused by an inadequate and fluctuating water supplies. More recent extinctions – of the Tasmanian tiger and several species of wallaby and bandicoot, for example – have been caused by humans.

Since their arrival in the late 18th century, European settlers have cleared and cultivated land in Australia, resulting in damage to more than 35 percent of the country's woodland, and the loss of up to 75 percent of the rainforest. Tree felling has led to soil erosion, and to the water table rising, which increases the salinity of the soil and destroys any trees left standing. New trees have been introduced but this has not helped: some of these cause further damage. The native pastures of Queensland, for example, have been turned into scrubland by the non-native prickly acacia.

Animal species that have been introduced have also wreaked havoc. The natural habitats of indigenous birds and marsupials have been disturbed by grazing cattle and sheep. Aggressive hunters such as the fox (introduced by European sportsmen as quarry) kill indigenous species, as well as the non-native rabbit. The cane toad, introduced as a pest-control measure, has itself turned into a pest.

The Great Barrier Reef lies off the coast of Queensland. The product of early changes in sea level followed by subsidence, this is one of the ecological wonders of the world. It is over 1,250 miles (2,000 km) long, with a total area of 135,100 square miles (350,000 sq km). It was made a World Heritage Site in 1981. As one of Australia's major tourist attractions government agencies and environmental groups are having to work hard to protect it from the ravages inflicted by its hundreds of thousands of visitors.

In 1999 the Australian government enacted the Environment Protection and Biodiversity Conservation Act, which introduced a comprehensive national protection scheme for wildlife. Rigorous assessment and approval is required for any building development likely to affect the habitats of threatened or migratory species. Time will tell whether these measures will reverse the decline of Australia's wildlife.

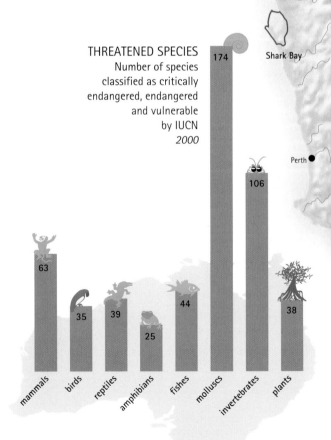

THREATENED SPECIES
Number of species classified as critically endangered, endangered and vulnerable by IUCN
2000

Shark Bay

Perth

mammals	birds	reptiles	amphibians	fishes	molluscs	invertebrates	plants
63	35	39	25	44	174	106	38

40

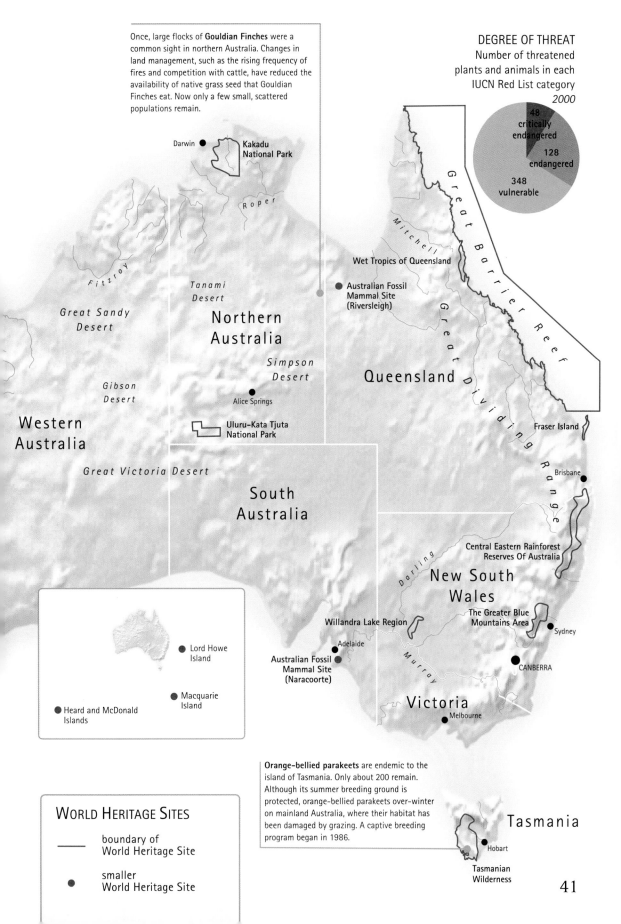

Once, large flocks of **Gouldian Finches** were a common sight in northern Australia. Changes in land management, such as the rising frequency of fires and competition with cattle, have reduced the availability of native grass seed that Gouldian Finches eat. Now only a few small, scattered populations remain.

DEGREE OF THREAT
Number of threatened plants and animals in each IUCN Red List category
2000

48 critically endangered

128 endangered

348 vulnerable

Darwin

Kakadu National Park

Roper

Fitzroy

Tanami Desert

Great Sandy Desert

Northern Australia

Wet Tropics of Queensland

Australian Fossil Mammal Site (Riversleigh)

Mitchell

Great Barrier Reef

Simpson Desert

Queensland

Great Dividing Range

Gibson Desert

Western Australia

Alice Springs

Uluru–Kata Tjuta National Park

Fraser Island

Great Victoria Desert

South Australia

Brisbane

Central Eastern Rainforest Reserves Of Australia

Darling

New South Wales

The Greater Blue Mountains Area

Sydney

Willandra Lake Region

Adelaide

Australian Fossil Mammal Site (Naracoorte)

Murray

CANBERRA

Victoria

Melbourne

Lord Howe Island

Macquarie Island

Heard and McDonald Islands

Orange–bellied parakeets are endemic to the island of Tasmania. Only about 200 remain. Although its summer breeding ground is protected, orange-bellied parakeets over-winter on mainland Australia, where their habitat has been damaged by grazing. A captive breeding program began in 1986.

Tasmania

Hobart

Tasmanian Wilderness

WORLD HERITAGE SITES

—— boundary of World Heritage Site

• smaller World Heritage Site

Central and South America is the most biologically diverse landmass in the world. It includes temperate and tropical forests, high-altitude desert plateau, and the glacial peaks of the Andes. While some areas remain relatively untouched by humans, others have been decimated by rapid urban growth. Last-ditch attempts are being made to save the Atlantic forests of Brazil, home to numerous species of plants and animals found nowhere else in the world, but reduced to less than 8 percent of their original size. Natural World Heritage Sites have been established throughout the continent but in 2001 three of these were on the "danger list" as a result of poor administration.

Important ecological areas do not fit neatly within political boundaries, and conservation projects are increasingly seeking co-operation between countries. In Central America, for example, where there are more than 400 protected areas, efforts are being made to establish a "Mesoamerican biological corridor" that integrates the efforts of eight countries. Although forest and mountain areas are now fairly well protected, more needs to be done to conserve wetland, coastal and marine areas. International co-operation is not always forthcoming. Attempts to protect the biologically rich mountainous Cordillera del Condor region in South America, for example, have been hampered by a border dispute between Ecuador and Peru.

It is important to protect the ecology of the high Andes region because its destruction or pollution would have an adverse effect on the water supply for the Amazon river. The Amazon basin itself contains the largest rainforest in the world and is home to several million species of plants, animals (including 3,000 species of fish) and micro-organisms, many of which remain unrecorded. The relatively stable climate, with high humidity and steady temperatures, has enabled species to adapt to local conditions and occupy very narrow environmental niches. The result is a large number of species, but a higher risk of a single species becoming extinct with the destruction of its own particular corner of the Amazon.

Indigenous peoples subsist in the Amazon by hunting, gathering and farming. Despite the luxuriant vegetation, the soils of the Amazon are sandy and infertile, so yields of staple crops such as cassava are low. This fragile food supply, coupled with the problems presented by moving through the forest, has given rise to small, diverse tribes living far apart from each other. The arrival of Europeans brought cattle ranching and the timber industry. Initially, settlement was restricted to the banks of the navigable rivers, still the principal means of transport, but the Trans-Amazon Highway, built in the 1960s, opened the interior of the Amazon to development. Once rainforest has been cleared for logging and to create pasture, it is prone to erosion. The extent of the loss of rainforest habitat is contested, but the latest estimates are that 14 percent of the total forest area was lost during the 20th century. In addition, mining effluent, which can contain mercury, has severely polluted parts of the Amazon River.

In 2001 the Brazilian Government announced an infrastructure program for the region, called "Advance Brazil" to encourage soya farming and its export. It includes plans for 6,250 miles (10,000 km) of new or upgraded roads through the rainforest, as well as canals to bypass the Amazon's rapids. Roads attract settlers and loggers, and substantially increase the risk of forest fires. Scientists predict that 42 percent of the rainforest could be denuded or degraded by 2020.

Opponents to the scheme argue that other, more sustainable, approaches to harnessing the resources of the Amazon could have been provided by eco-tourism, sensitive forestry and the study of practical uses for natural products and the genetic information contained in the region's wildlife. Loss of this habitat will not only exacerbate global warming, as the rainforest goes up in smoke, it will also deny Brazil an opportunity to sell "carbon credits" to industrialized countries unwilling to reduce their domestic emissions of carbon dioxide.

Whale Sanctuary of El Vizcaino

MEXICO

CUBA

DOMINICAN REPUBLIC

Sian Ka'an
Barrier–Reef Reserve System
Tikal National Park
GUATEMALA
EL SALVADOR
HONDURAS
NICARAGUA
JAMAICA
BELIZE
HAITI

Río Platano Biosphere Reserve

Morne Trois Pitons National Park
DOMINICA

Area De Conservación Guanacaste
COSTA RICA
Darien National Park
Los Katios National Park
PANAMA

COCOS ISLAND

Cocos Island National Park

GALAPAGOS ISLANDS

Galapagos Islands

VENEZUELA

COLOMBIA

ECUADOR

Sangay National Park

PERU

Huascarán National Park

Manu National Park

Noel Kempff Mercado National Park

BOLIVIA

TRINIDAD & TOBAGO

GUYANA

SURINAME

Canaima National Park

Central Suriname Nature Reserve

B R A Z I L

Jaú National Park

Panatal Conservation Area

Discovery Coast Atlantic Forest Reserves

Atlantic Forest Southeast Reserves

PARAGUAY

Iguacu National Park
Iguazu National Park

CHILE

URUGUAY

ARGENTINA

Península Valdés

Los Glaciares

PROTECTED LAND

Percentage of total land area protected under IUCN categories I-V *1997*

- 36% – 45%
- 21% – 35%
- 11% – 20%
- 1% – 10%
- under 1.0%
- none or no data
- ● World Heritage Site
- ◉ World Heritage Site on danger list in *2001*

Around 55% of the trees and 80% of the primates found in Brazil's Atlantic forest, including the **muriqui**, are endemic to the area.

It is predicted that the proposed new road from Cuiabá to Santarem will carry 20 million tons of crops to the river, and that it will create a corridor of development up to 60 miles (100 km) wide.

In 1998 and 1999 **fires** ravaged the Amazon. They destroyed 30% of crops in the Brazilian state of Roraima and threatened indigenous Indian villages.

COLOMBIA

ECUADOR

PERU

Boa Vista

Macapá

Belém

Rio Amazonas

Manaus

Santarém

Maraba

Humaitá
Pôrto Velho

BRAZIL

Rio Branco

Rio Tapajós

Brasília

BOLIVIA

Cuiabá

The **Tapajos National Park**, set up in 1974, covers about 3,860 square miles (10,000 sq km) of dense tropical rain forest, home to abundant wildlife. The proposal to upgrade the Trans-Amazon highway is bound to have a derimental effect on the ecology of the park.

AMAZON BASIN

- IUCN Protected Areas categories I – VI
- Tapajos National Park
- existing road
- proposed upgraded road

GALAPAGOS ISLANDS

The Galapagos Islands lie in the Pacific Ocean, about 625 miles (1,000 km) off the coast of South America. Because these volcanic islands have risen out of the seabed, evolution has taken place in isolation from the mainland, giving rise to species endemic to the islands. As Charles Darwin realized after his visit in 1835, species on neighbouring islands within the group have evolved unique characteristics in response to their environment. The result is small, localized populations that are vulnerable to habitat destruction, disease, or climate change.

"Galapagos" means "tortoise" in Spanish, and the islands are home to giant tortoises, as well as about 300,000 marine iguanas. In the absence of traditional predators – rice rats and two species of bat are the only native mammals – seabirds breed freely and colonies of boobies, frigate birds, and the rare lava gull flourish on the islands. In 1959 Ecuador declared the Galapagos a national park and in 1978 the islands became the first United Nations' World Heritage Site.

Some of the islands have been settled by humans, and the population had reached over 16,000 in 2001. Settlers have imported around 500 species of plants, which are displacing the native flora, as well as non-native animals, such as goats, which compete for grazing land with the giant tortoises.

Tourism is the mainstay of the islands' economy, with over 60,000 tourists visiting each year. Fishing is also important, with at least 800 fishermen based on the islands. Large, commercial boats also fish offshore, creating a hazard to marine mammals and birds.

Prompted by Unesco's threat to place the Galapagos on the World Heritage in Danger list, Ecuador issued an emergency decree in 1997 restricting the introduction of alien species, and promoting conservation. In 1998 Ecuador expanded the islands' no-fishing zone from 15 to 40 nautical miles offshore. However, attempts to limit fishing have met with local resistance. Park wardens have been shot, giant tortoises taken hostage and a research station damaged. The fate of the islands' wildlife hangs on whether both local and conservational needs can be met.

The **Galapagos penguin** is at risk. These penguins eat fish, abundant in the cold, nutrient-rich waters around the islands. Many suffered as a result of the El Niño phenomenon in 1997–98, when warmer seas disrupted the penguins' food supply.

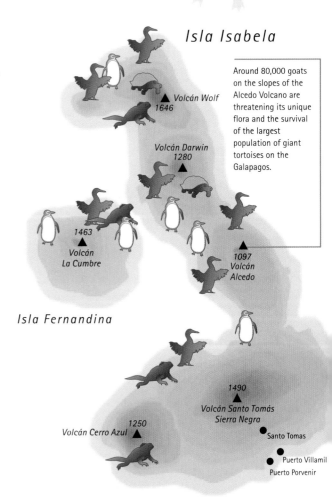

Isla Isabela

Around 80,000 goats on the slopes of the Alcedo Volcano are threatening its unique flora and the survival of the largest population of giant tortoises on the Galapagos.

Volcán Wolf
1646

Volcán Darwin
1280

1463
Volcán
La Cumbre

1097
Volcán
Alcedo

Isla Fernandina

1490
Volcán Santo Tomás
Sierra Negra

1250
Volcán Cerro Azul

Santo Tomas

Puerto Villamil
Puerto Porvenir

Found only on the Galapagos, the **lava gull**, with 300 to 400 breeding pairs, is considered the rarest gull in the world.

Isla Pinta

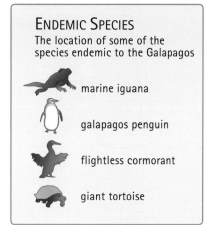
Isla Marchena

Isla Genovesa

The **giant tortoise**, once numerous on the islands,
presented an easy meal to passing sailors and
three of the 14 known subspecies became extinct.
In recent times, the main threat to the tortoise
has been the domestic goat, which competes with
it for grazing. Captive-breeding projects have been
running since the mid-1960s. These are too late,
however, for "Lonesome George", the sole
remaining tortoise from the island of Pinta.

GIANT TORTOISE
Estimated number
of individuals in
1535 and *2000*

250,000   **15,000**

1535   *2000*

Isla San Salvador

Isla Rábida

Isla Santa Cruz

Isla Pinzón

On 16 January 2001, the oil tanker
Jessica, carrying 160,000 gallons of
diesel and 80,000 gallons of bunker
fuel, ran aground off San Cristóbal
Island. Her tanks ruptured. Fortunately,
winds and currents took the oil away
from the island, preventing a major
ecological disaster.

Since 1970 more
than 500 young
tortoises, bred in
captivity, have
been released on
the island of
Pinzon.

● Puerto Ayora

Isla Santa Fé

Puerto Baquerizo Moreno ● ● El Progreso

Isla San Cristóbal

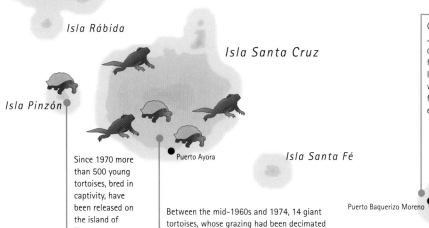

Between the mid-1960s and 1974, 14 giant
tortoises, whose grazing had been decimated
by goats, were taken from Española to
breeding pens on Santa Cruz island. The goats
were eventually removed from the island and
by March 2000 a total of 1,000 tortoises had
been reintroduced to the island.

Puerto Velasco Ibarra ●

Isla Santa María

Isla Española

MADAGASCAR

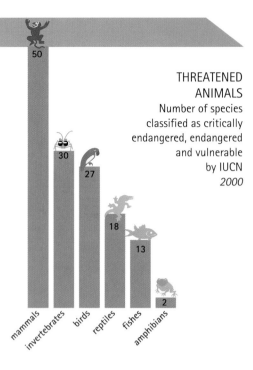

Madagascar is the world's fourth largest island, with a land area of approximately 226,000 square miles (582,000 sq km). It is thought to have separated from Gondwanaland (present-day Africa) 60 million years ago.

Madagascar's geographical isolation has led to separate evolution, producing many endemic species and a diverse range of habitat: tropical conditions along the coast, temperate inland areas and arid deserts in the south.

Several of Madagascar's endemic species are threatened, despite the government's endorsement of international agreements on biodiversity, desertification, endangered species, and marine life conservation. With a human population exceeding 14 million and growing at an annual rate of nearly 3 percent, the pressure on the country's natural habitats is likely to continue.

Although the great elephantbird and Delalande's coua, or snail-eating coua, are known to have become extinct, new species are being discovered all the time. A new species of woolly lemur, five new dwarf lemurs and three more species of mouse lemur were all announced at the end of 2000, bringing the total number of known lemur species to sixty-one.

THREATENED ANIMALS
Number of species classified as critically endangered, endangered and vulnerable by IUCN
2000

- 50 mammals
- 30 invertebrates
- 27 birds
- 18 reptiles
- 13 fishes
- 2 amphibians

DEGREE OF THREAT
Number of animals in each IUCN Red List category
2000

- 4 extinct
- 21 critically endangered
- 45 endangered
- 74 vulnerable
- 5 conservation dependent
- 36 near threatened status

THREATENED PLANT SPECIES
Number of threatened plants
2000

- 0 extinct
- 19 possibly extinct
- 93 endangered
- 57 vulnerable
- 90 rare
- 64 indeterminate

The **Madagascar rosy periwinkle** is the source of two alkaloids — vincristine and vinblastine — used to treat (and usually cure) childhood leukaemia. The plants from which the alkaloids are extracted are now grown elsewhere. The drug industry has not returned any benefit to the people or to conservation projects in Madagascar.

Cap d'Ambre

Antsiranana

Forêt d'Ambre

Montagne d'Ambre

Analamerana

Ankarana

Iharana

Lokobe

Tsaratanana

Manongarlvo

Andapa

Marojejy

Bora

Anjanaharibe-Sud

Antalaha

Mahajanga

Sofia

Masoala

Nosy Mangabe

Marovoay

Katsepy

Ankarafantsika

Cap Saint-André

Tampoketsa Analamaitso

Mananara

Baie Baly/Soalaid

Lac Kinkony

Tsingy de Namoroka

Marotandrano

Ambalovaky

Lac Alaotra

Maningozo

Fenoarivo Atsinanana

Bemarivo

Manambaho

Katsijy

Zahamena

Mahavay

Ikopa

Betsiboka

Betampona

Ambohijanahary

Toamasina

Ambohitartely

Mangerivola

Bemaraha

Mantadia

Manambolo

Antananarivo

Lac Bemamba

Antsirabe

Lac Itasy

Mangoro

Kirindy

Morondava

Ancranomena

Ranomafana

Kirindy / Belo Sur Mer

Fianarantsoa

Mananjary

Mangoky

ombe

Lac Ihotry

Andringîtra

Zombitse

Isalo

Andrevo

Vohibasia

Onilahy

Pic de Ivohibe

Toliara

Manombo

Beza-Mahafaly

Kalambatritra

Tsimanampetsotsa

Andohahela

Hatokaliotsy

Taolanaro

Lac Anony

Cap Sainte-Marie

The **fish eagle** was common in north-west Madagascar until the 1930s. It is now very rare, as a result of persecution, hunting, and the loss of nesting and feeding habitat.

The **golden lemur**, or golden bamboo lemur, has a range restricted to south-eastern Madagascar. About 1,000 inhabit the Ranomafana National Park. They live in rain forest, eating the base of bamboo leaves and all new growth. The young bamboo shoots eaten by the golden lemur are toxic and lethal to most other mammals.

Tsingy de Bermaraha Strict Nature Reserve is a World Heritage Site. Endangered lemurs and birds thrive in the undisturbed forests, lakes and mangrove swamps.

PROTECTED AREAS IN MADAGASCAR

⭐ Strict Nature Reserve

⭐ National Park

● Habitat Species Management Area

● Managed Resource Protected Area

47

ENDANGERED ANIMALS AND PLANTS

4

"Thousands of cooking pots across Africa are simmering away with cuts of gorilla and chimp in them."

— Sam Kanyamibwa,
World Conservation Monitoring Centre, Rwanda

Apes, humans, monkeys, and prosimians such as lorises, bush babies, and lemurs make up the 234 species of Primates, a mammalian Order with distinctive common features indicating descent from a single ancestor: a small, tree-dwelling mammal that subsisted primarily on insects.

Primates have prehensile hands with opposable thumbs, large brains (especially the cerebral cortex), and usually bear single offspring. Most are well adapted to life in trees, especially tropical forests, although some species have become terrestrial. Primates tend to live in complex social groups, and as infants are dependent on their mother, both for sustanance and for lessons in the practical and social skills. With a few exceptions, such as the Japanese macaque that lives on the Shimokita Peninsula at a latitude of 41°N, very few primates have colonized temperate areas because they need a supply of food during the winter months as well as long daylight hours for foraging.

All primates share behavioral and anatomical characteristics, but humans and chimpanzees are particularly close. Chimps share almost 99 percent of our DNA. They use tools, laugh when tickled, and – when allowed – can live for 60 years. Like many other species of primate, chimps are endangered by deforestation and, especially, its consequences: as logging companies open up the forests, hunters move in. Since the mid-1980s hunting for "bushmeat" has become a lucrative industry. In 2001, over a million tonnes was taken from the Congo basin alone.

A hundred years ago there were some two million chimps living in the Central African rainforest, stretching from Sierra Leone to Tanzania. In 2001 only 200,000 remained; at the current rates of decline they all could perish by 2010.

Our closest relatives are the four great apes: **gorilla**, chimpanzee, bonobo (pygmy chimpanzee), and orang-utan.

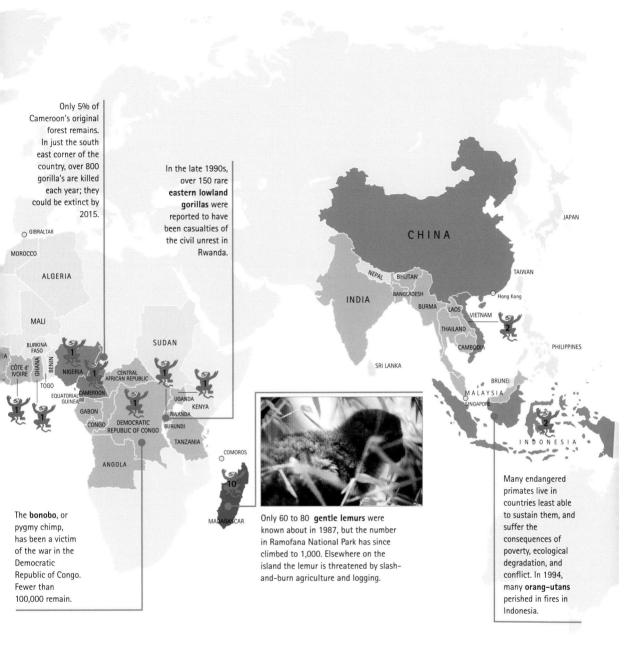

Only 5% of Cameroon's original forest remains. In just the south east corner of the country, over 800 gorilla's are killed each year; they could be extinct by 2015.

In the late 1990s, over 150 rare **eastern lowland gorillas** were reported to have been casualties of the civil unrest in Rwanda.

GIBRALTAR

MOROCCO

ALGERIA

MALI

BURKINA FASO

CÔTE d' IVOIRE

GHANA

BENIN

TOGO

NIGERIA

EQUATORIAL GUINEA

CAMEROON

GABON

CONGO

CENTRAL AFRICAN REPUBLIC

DEMOCRATIC REPUBLIC OF CONGO

SUDAN

UGANDA

RWANDA

BURUNDI

KENYA

TANZANIA

ANGOLA

COMOROS

MADAGASCAR

CHINA

JAPAN

TAIWAN

NEPAL

BHUTAN

BANGLADESH

INDIA

BURMA

LAOS

VIETNAM

THAILAND

CAMBODIA

Hong Kong

PHILIPPINES

SRI LANKA

BRUNEI

MALAYSIA

SINGAPORE

INDONESIA

The **bonobo**, or pygmy chimp, has been a victim of the war in the Democratic Republic of Congo. Fewer than 100,000 remain.

Only 60 to 80 **gentle lemurs** were known about in 1987, but the number in Ramofana National Park has since climbed to 1,000. Elsewhere on the island the lemur is threatened by slash-and-burn agriculture and logging.

Many endangered primates live in countries least able to sustain them, and suffer the consequences of poverty, ecological degradation, and conflict. In 1994, many **orang-utans** perished in fires in Indonesia.

About 90 percent of **primates** live in tropical forests. They play an integral role in the ecology of their habitat, helping to pollinate plants and disperse seeds.

THREATENED PRIMATES
Number of species of primates classified as critically endangered, endangered or vulnerable *2000*

- more than 25
- 11 – 25
- 4 – 10
- 1 – 3
- none or no data

number of primates classified as critically endangered

51

BIG CATS

Big cats belong to the *Felidae* family – a group of carnivorous mammals that includes the cheetah in addition to "true" cats: the lion, tiger, jaguar, leopard, puma, and the domestic cat.

Cats, whether large or small, are built for performance and are more specialized in this respect than any other flesh-eating mammal. They are powerfully built animals, with large and highly developed brains, making them more intelligent as well as stronger than their prey. They are also so well-coordinated that they almost always land on their feet when they fall.

Although the lion, tiger, and cheetah are agile climbers, they are mainly terrestrial in habit. The leopard, jaguar, and ocelot, in contrast, are very much at home in trees, where they sometimes sleep. The larger cats range over wide areas, often up to 50 square miles (129 sq km). Big cats usually rove alone or with a companion. African lions do form prides, but these loosely bound groups of females, cubs and a single adult male, lack the rigid hierarchy found in dog and wolf packs.

Humans are the main threat to big cats and hunting has long been a popular pastime. It remains a lucrative sport: in Botswana, for example, recreational hunters may pay up to US $30,000 to shoot a lion. The skin, teeth and claws of big cats provide rich pickings for traders. Those not threatened by hunters have had their extensive territories steadily eroded by agriculture and human settlement.

Many of Asia's big cats are under threat, including the snow leopard (reduced to around 6,000 in the wild), the Siberian tiger (reduced to 400 in the wild) and the Amur leopard (see page 95). As wild populations of big cats decline towards extinction, zoos and other sanctuaries become even more vital in ensuring their survival.

CANADA

UNITED STATES OF AMERICA

MEXICO

The highly endangered **Florida Panther** is making its last stand in the higher elevations in the swamps of the Everglades. The few remaining animals became highly inbred, causing such genetic flaws as heart defects and sterility. In the 1990s, closely related panthers from Texas were released in Florida and are successfully breeding with the Florida panthers. Increased genetic variation and protection of habitat may yet save this subspecies.

SENEGAL
GAMBIA
GUINEA-BISSAU

SIE
LE

PERU

BOLIVIA

CHILE   ARGENTINA

The **cheetah** is generally considered the speediest of animals, capable of 60-70 mph (100-110 kmph), with rare reports of even higher speeds. A cheetah may also pursue its prey for a considerable distance, as much as 3.5 miles (5.5 km). But even its speed may not save it from hunters and the threat of extinction.

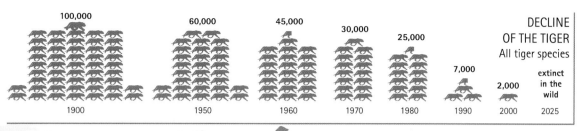

DECLINE OF THE TIGER
All tiger species

100,000	60,000	45,000	30,000	25,000	7,000	2,000	extinct in the wild
1900	1950	1960	1970	1980	1990	2000	2025

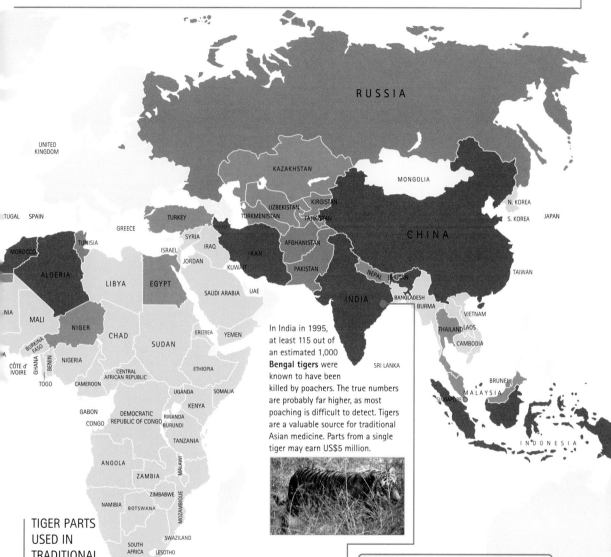

In India in 1995, at least 115 out of an estimated 1,000 **Bengal tigers** were known to have been killed by poachers. The true numbers are probably far higher, as most poaching is difficult to detect. Tigers are a valuable source for traditional Asian medicine. Parts from a single tiger may earn US$5 million.

TIGER PARTS USED IN TRADITIONAL MEDICINE

brain
laziness, pimples

eyeballs
epilepsy, malaria, fevers, cataracts, convulsions

claws
as a sedative

nose
epilepsy, convulsions, dog bites

whiskers
toothache

blood
constitution, willpower

testes
tuberculosis of the lymph nodes

tail
skin diseases

teeth
fever, rabies, asthma, sores on the penis

stomach
stomach upsets

fat
leprosy, rheumatism

bones
rheumatism, weakness, paralysis

feces
boils, piles

flesh
nausea, malaria, improves vitality, tones stomach and spleen

THREATENED CATS
Number of species of big cats classified as critically endangered, endangered or vulnerable *2000*

- 5 or more
- 4
- 3
- 2
- 1
- none or no data

53

UNGULATES

Horses, deer, cattle, sheep and goats are all ungulates — mammals with hooves of hard skin that allow the animals to run. Elephants and rhinoceroses (see pages 56-57) are also ungulates. Their teeth are adapted for their plant diet, with strong molars for grinding. Preyed upon by big cats, wolves and other carnivores, ungulates rely on various methods of defence. Some are large, many are swift, and others grow horns or antlers. They often mass in large herds to minimize the risk to an individual.

Domesticated ungulates accompanied earlier European explorers to Australia and to isolated islands all over the world, but have often threatened indigenous herbivores by over-grazing native plants. Non-native ungulates have interbred with indigenous species, and have also transmitted diseases such as rinderpest, which spreads from cattle to wild buffalo in Southeast Asia.

Ungulates provide an important source of meat for humans, and their hides are used for clothing and shelter. As vehicles and guns improved during the 20th century, ungulate populations began to suffer from the over-hunting that remains the most serious threat to their survival today.

Areas designated as reserves are often vital for ungulate conservation. The tourists flocking to witness herds of ungulates roaming over African plains, provide a potential source of income for conservation in reserves. Kruger National Park in South Africa is Africa's oldest reserve, founded in 1898, while Tanzania boasts the Serengeti and Ngorongoro parks.

To secure local support for conservation inside and outside reserves local people must enjoy the profits from hunting and tourism and participate in the management of their wildlife. The Communal Area Management Programme for Indigenous Resources (CAMPFIRE) in Zimbabwe is a successful example, demonstrating that the managed re-introduction of ungulates to areas where they had been hunted to local extinction can be successful with proper enforcement against poaching.

CANADA

UNITED STATES OF AMERICA

MEXICO

BELIZE
GUATEMALA   HONDURAS
NICARAGUA
COSTA RICA
PANAMA   VENEZUELA
COLOMBIA
ECUADOR

PERU
BRAZIL
BOLIVIA
PARAGUAY
CHILE
ARGENTINA

WESTERN SAHARA
MAURITAN
SENEGAL —
GAMBIA —
GUINEA-BISSAU—
SIERRA LEONE——
LIBERIA——

There may have been 60 million **bison** in North America before the arrival of Europeans. Hunting drove the bison to the point of extinction as settlers swept west across the continent. About 1,500 survived in areas such as Yellowstone National Park, established in 1872. The number of bison has since risen to over 350,000, most reared commercially for meat, hide and other products.

CHANGING FORTUNES OF THE NORTH AMERICAN BISON

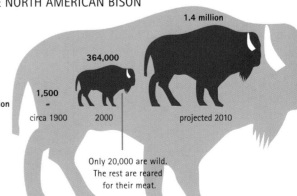

1.4 million

364,000

1,500

30 – 60 million
circa 1800

circa 1900

2000

projected 2010

Only 20,000 are wild. The rest are reared for their meat.

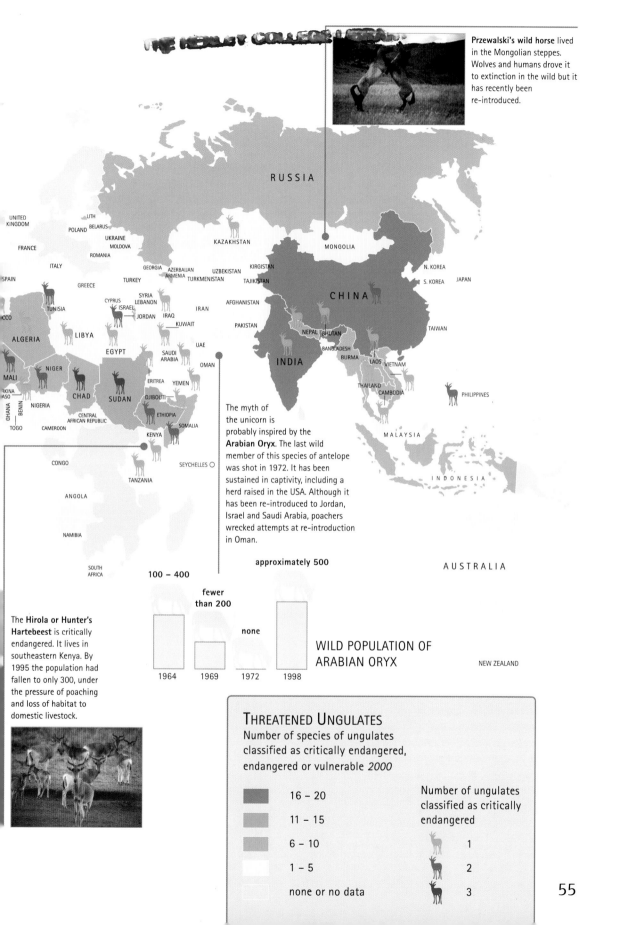

Przewalski's wild horse lived in the Mongolian steppes. Wolves and humans drove it to extinction in the wild but it has recently been re-introduced.

RUSSIA

UNITED KINGDOM
LITH
POLAND BELARUS
FRANCE
UKRAINE
MOLDOVA
KAZAKHSTAN
MONGOLIA
ITALY
ROMANIA
SPAIN
GEORGIA AZERBAIJAN
ARMENIA
GREECE
TURKEY
UZBEKISTAN
KIRGISTAN
N. KOREA
S. KOREA
JAPAN
TURKMENISTAN
TAJIKISTAN
CYPRUS
SYRIA
LEBANON
ISRAEL
TUNISIA
JORDAN IRAQ
IRAN
AFGHANISTAN
CHINA
KUWAIT
CCO
ALGERIA
LIBYA
PAKISTAN
TAIWAN
EGYPT
UAE
SAUDI ARABIA
NEPAL BHUTAN
NIGER
OMAN
BANGLADESH
BURMA
INDIA
LAOS VIETNAM
MALI
CHAD
SUDAN
ERITREA
YEMEN
THAILAND
RKINA ASO
DJIBOUTI
CAMBODIA
GHANA
BENIN
NIGERIA
CENTRAL AFRICAN REPUBLIC
ETHIOPIA
PHILIPPINES
TOGO
CAMEROON
SOMALIA
KENYA
CONGO
SEYCHELLES
MALAYSIA
TANZANIA
ANGOLA
INDONESIA
NAMIBIA

The myth of the unicorn is probably inspired by the **Arabian Oryx**. The last wild member of this species of antelope was shot in 1972. It has been sustained in captivity, including a herd raised in the USA. Although it has been re-introduced to Jordan, Israel and Saudi Arabia, poachers wrecked attempts at re-introduction in Oman.

SOUTH AFRICA

AUSTRALIA

100 – 400

approximately 500

fewer than 200

WILD POPULATION OF ARABIAN ORYX

NEW ZEALAND

| 1964 | 1969 | 1972 | 1998 |

The **Hirola or Hunter's Hartebeest** is critically endangered. It lives in southeastern Kenya. By 1995 the population had fallen to only 300, under the pressure of poaching and loss of habitat to domestic livestock.

THREATENED UNGULATES
Number of species of ungulates classified as critically endangered, endangered or vulnerable *2000*

	16 – 20
	11 – 15
	6 – 10
	1 – 5
	none or no data

Number of ungulates classified as critically endangered

	1
	2
	3

55

The elephant family comprises two species: the Indian elephant (*Elephas maximus*), weighing about 5.5 tonnes, and the African elephant (*Loxodonta africana*) weighing up to 7.5 tons and standing between 10 and 12 feet (3–4 m) at the shoulder. Both species live in habitats ranging from thick jungle to savanna. They form small family groups led by the eldest females, and where food is plentiful groups join to create larger herds. Most bulls live in bachelor herds apart from the cows. Elephants migrate seasonally, according to the availability of food and water. They spend many hours eating and may consume 500 lbs (225 kg) of grasses and other vegetation in a day.

For many centuries the Indian elephant has been used as both a ceremonial and draft animal. Elephants have been crucial to Southeast Asian logging operations, for example. African elephants are also used as working animals, but not as extensively.

Elephants are in great danger from habitat destruction and human exploitation. Both Indian and African elephants are classified as endangered; the African elephant suffers in particular from poaching for the ivory trade. Although conservation measures have been taken, including patrols to protect against poachers, and the creation of large reserves, these can lead to further problems. In good conditions, elephant populations can increase at a rate of 5 percent a year which leads to overpopulation and may make culling necessary. Corridor areas are vital to protect major migratory routes and to prevent herds from becoming isolated.

Rhinoceroses have one or two horns on the upper surface of the snout, composed of keratin, a fibrous protein found in hair. The Indian rhinoceros (*R. unicornis*) is the largest of the family, at about 14 feet (4.3 m) long and weighing up to 5 tons. Most rhinoceroses are solitary inhabitants of savanna, scrub forest, or marsh, although the Sumatran rhino is now found only in deep forest. Rhinoceroses have poor eyesight but acute hearing and sense of smell. Despite their bulk, they are remarkably agile; the black rhino may attain a speed of about 30 mph (45 kmph), even in thick brush.

All but the white rhinoceros are listed as endangered in the Red Data Book. Despite protective laws, poaching continues to supply a thriving market, with rhinoceros horn and blood among the most highly-prized ingredients in traditional medicines: rhino horns can fetch as much as US $60,000 per kilogram.

Captive-breeding programs offer the only hope for maintaining some species until adequate protection can be provided in the wild.

The **Indian elephant** is more closely related to the extinct mammoth than to the African elephant.

Mammoths are members of an extinct genus of elephants. The woolly Northern, or Siberian, mammoth is by far the best-known of all mammoths. Famished after the end of the Ice Age (11,000 years ago) by a diet of low-nutrient mosses, and increasingly harried by human hunters, the big grazers dwindled to extinction. Siberian mammoths were sometimes trapped in ice crevasses. Their bodies became remarkably well preserved in the ice and attempts are now underway to collect viable DNA from these beasts in the hope of being able to resurrect the species.

The **Javan rhino** is the rarest of the rhino species, with fewer than 60 animals surviving in only two known locations: one in Indonesia and the other in Vietnam. Rhinos have been poached from these small populations in recent years and much more intensive protection is needed if this species is to survive.

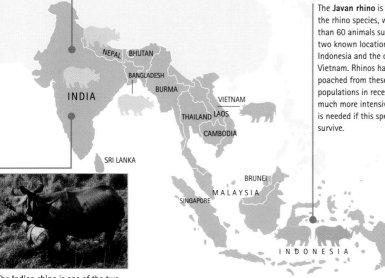

NEPAL BHUTAN
BANGLADESH
BURMA
INDIA
VIETNAM
THAILAND LAOS
CAMBODIA
SRI LANKA
BRUNEI
MALAYSIA
SINGAPORE
INDONESIA

The **Indian rhino** is one of the two greatest success stories in rhino conservation (the other being the southern white rhino in South Africa). With strict protection from Indian and Nepalese wildlife authorities, Indian rhino numbers have recovered from under 200 earlier in this century to over 2,500. Poaching has, however, remained high and the success of conservation efforts is precarious without continued and increased support from the governments in India and Nepal.

DISTRIBUTION OF ELEPHANTS AND RHINOS *2000*

Indian elephant	
African elephant	
African elephant recently extinct	
no native elephants	

Number of rhinos, where known

25	White rhino
25	Black rhino
	Sumatran rhino
	Indian rhino
	Javan rhino

57

BEARS

Bears are among the largest of the carnivores and belong to the family *Ursidae*. Nine species are recognized, including the lesser panda (sometimes classified as a raccoon), and there are numerous subspecies. Six species are listed as threatened. Insufficient data exist about the sun or honey bear but this species is also feared to be threatened.

Bears vary in size from the sun bear, weighing only 66 lbs (30 kg), to the Kodiak brown bear, which can weigh 1,540 lbs (700 kg). Their diet varies as well. Polar bears are particularly fond of seals, panda bears eat mainly bamboo, and sloth bears prefer insects. Most bears, of course, eat honey.

Bears tend to live solitary lives, pairing only to mate. They are strong swimmers and smaller species are agile climbers.

Bears are hunted as trophies, for their hides, for meat and also from fear. When their territory overlaps with cultivated land, they are perceived as pests. Poachers kill bears for body parts and trap them for the pet trade or for use as performing animals. Bear gallbladders are used in traditional Chinese medicine to cure liver disease, cancer and other ailments.

In many parts of the world bears' habitats have been eroded and their populations fragmented, leading to the threat of local extinction. Small, insular groups of bears can also become weakened by genetic depletion.

Sophisticated management of hunting and habitat protection has sustained bear species living in North America and the Arctic, although pollution and global warming are serious problems (see pages 36-37). Resources for conservation in Asia and South America are not as plentiful, however, and a growing human population demands more land, which inevitably threaten bears. The establishment of wildlife "corridors" between reserves allows bears from different populations to mate and mix genes. Captive-breeding programs also offer hope for endangered bears. Over 100 giant pandas are kept in the world's zoos, but captivity impedes their breeding success rate as well as their life span.

The **brown bear**, called "grizzly" in North America, once ranged over all the northern continents. It has been hunted near to extinction in Europe, where only isolated populations totalling 13,000 remain in mountain ranges, and the 100 or so left in the Pyrenees are probably doomed.

The **spectacled bear** is found in South America, living in terrains ranging from desert to rain forest, but it thrives best in cloud forest at around 2,000 metres. Logging and mining activites, and the expansion of agricultural land, is threatening the bear's survival. It is also hunted for its meat and skin. Attempts at conservation are hampered by unstable political environments and by drug trafficking.

VENEZUELA
COLOMBIA
ECUADOR
PERU
BRAZIL
BOLIVIA
ARGENTINA

There are fewer than 1,000 **giant pandas** left in the wild. They live in mountain bamboo forests in central China, where the government has declared 33 panda reserves. Logging and forest clearance for agriculture threatens the remaining panda habitat outside these reserves. Poaching is a threat and the giant panda's slow rate of reproduction jeopardizes its chances of recovery.

THREATENED PANDAS
Species of panda considered under threat *2000*

Lesser Panda

Giant Panda

The Baluchistan bear, a subspecies of the **Asiatic black bear**, is critically endangered.

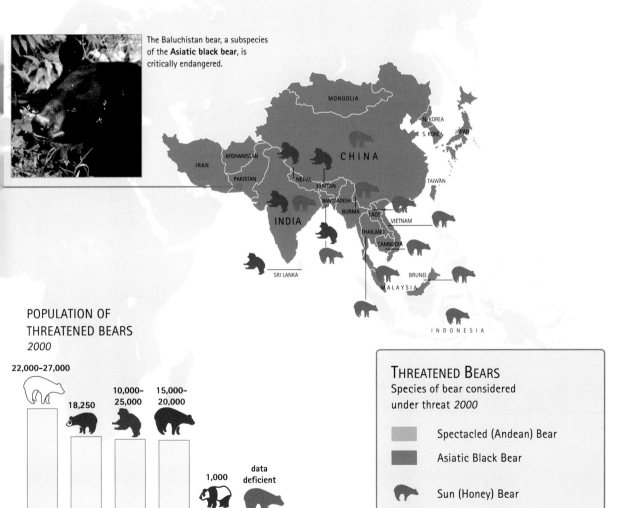

POPULATION OF THREATENED BEARS
2000

22,000–27,000

18,250

10,000–25,000

15,000–20,000

1,000

data deficient

polar bear | spectacled bear | sloth bear | Asiatic black bear | giant panda | sun bear

THREATENED BEARS
Species of bear considered under threat *2000*

Spectacled (Andean) Bear

Asiatic Black Bear

Sun (Honey) Bear

Sloth Bear

RODENTS

There are over 2,000 species of rodent, making them the most diverse order of mammals. They are found above and below ground and in all parts of the world except for New Zealand and the Antarctic. Most rodents are small – the dormouse weighs less than an ounce (20 grams) – although there are exceptions, such as the capybara of South America, which grows to 110 lbs (50 kg).

Rodents are commonly seen as agricultural pests, carriers of disease such as bubonic plague and as a threat to biodiversity. The black rat and Norway rat are cited as key villains, travelling all over the world via ships, wrecking food stores and displacing native rodent species. In fact, rodents are ecologically valuable. Some, such as squirrels, help plants to reproduce by burying seeds. Burrowing rodents mix, fertilize and aerate soil. As prey, rodents provide essential food for predators.

Rodent populations tend to be larger than those of other groups of mammals and their breeding rates are very high, making them well-equipped as a species to recover from adverse weather and epidemics. Despite this advantage, sustained pressure on rodent populations can cause local extermination; for species with only a limited range this can result in extinction.

The greatest threat to rodents is the progressive loss of their natural habitat from urbanization, cultivation of crops, and grazing of domestic livestock. Throughout the 20th century the US government sponsored a program of poisoning and plowing to eliminate prairie dogs, which degrade cattle-grazing land. As a result, the black-footed ferret, which preyed on the prairie dogs, disappeared. Although still classified as extinct in the wild, black-footed ferrets have been reintroduced with some success from a captive-bred population.

Fur trapping is illegal in many places, but continues to threaten some rodent species. Rarity and value tend to go hand in hand, thus encouraging trapping of the few remaining animals.

Colony of Vancouver Island Marmots

A MARMOT ON THE BRINK
Number of Vancouver Island Marmots in the wild

235 — 1984
102 — 1997
71 — 1998
57 — 1999

CANADA

UNITED STATES OF AMERICA

MEXICO
GUATEMALA
HONDURAS
COSTA RICA
PANAMA
BAHAMAS
CUBA
JAMAICA HAITI
DOMINICAN REPUBLIC

ST VINCENT & THE GRENADINES
VENEZUELA GUYANA
SURINAME
FRENCH GUIANA (Fr)
COLOMBIA
ECUADOR
PERU
BRAZIL
BOLIVIA
PARAGUAY
CHILE
ARGENTINA

PORTUGAL SPAIN
MOROCCO
MAURITA
SENEGA
BELG
FRA

North American beavers dam rivers to create wetlands, providing habitat for a wide range of other animals. They were almost driven to extinction by fur trappers and land drainage in the early 20th century.

The population of the **short-tailed chinchilla** collapsed by 80% in the last decade of the 20th century due to depletion of its habitat in the mountains of South America, and illegal trapping for its valuable fur. It is now critically endangered.

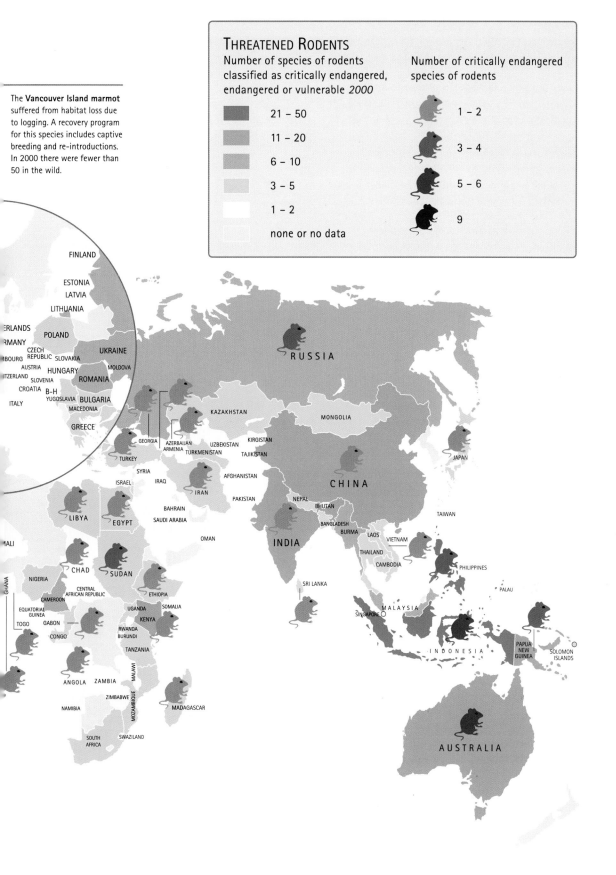

The **Vancouver Island marmot** suffered from habitat loss due to logging. A recovery program for this species includes captive breeding and re-introductions. In 2000 there were fewer than 50 in the wild.

THREATENED RODENTS

Number of species of rodents classified as critically endangered, endangered or vulnerable *2000*

- 21 – 50
- 11 – 20
- 6 – 10
- 3 – 5
- 1 – 2
- none or no data

Number of critically endangered species of rodents

- 1 – 2
- 3 – 4
- 5 – 6
- 9

FINLAND
ESTONIA
LATVIA
LITHUANIA
ERLANDS
RMANY
POLAND
CZECH
BOURG REPUBLIC SLOVAKIA UKRAINE
AUSTRIA
ITZERLAND SLOVENIA HUNGARY MOLDOVA
CROATIA ROMANIA
ITALY B-H
YUGOSLAVIA BULGARIA
MACEDONIA
GREECE
GEORGIA
AZERBAIJAN
TURKEY ARMENIA TURKMENISTAN
SYRIA
ISRAEL IRAQ
AFGHANISTAN
IRAN
LIBYA PAKISTAN
EGYPT
BAHRAIN
SAUDI ARABIA
OMAN
MALI
NIGERIA CHAD SUDAN
CENTRAL
AFRICAN REPUBLIC ETHIOPIA
CAMEROON
EQUATORIAL UGANDA SOMALIA
GUINEA KENYA
TOGO GABON
CONGO RWANDA
BURUNDI
TANZANIA
ANGOLA ZAMBIA MALAWI
ZIMBABWE
NAMIBIA MADAGASCAR
MOZAMBIQUE
SOUTH SWAZILAND
AFRICA

RUSSIA
KAZAKHSTAN
MONGOLIA
UZBEKISTAN
KIRGISTAN
TAJIKISTAN
CHINA
JAPAN
NEPAL
BHUTAN TAIWAN
BANGLADESH
INDIA BURMA LAOS
THAILAND VIETNAM
CAMBODIA PHILIPPINES
SRI LANKA PALAU
SINGAPORE MALAYSIA
INDONESIA PAPUA
NEW
GUINEA SOLOMON
ISLANDS
AUSTRALIA

BATS

There are about 900 species of bats, nearly a third of which are threatened. Bats are the only flying mammals. Most eat insects, although some eat nectar and fruit, helping to pollinate plants and disperse seeds. Vampire bats in Central and South America feed on the blood of large mammals.

Bats are nocturnal, avoiding the heat of the day, the risk of dehydration and the attentions of predators. They navigate at night using a form of sonar or echo-location. By day they roost in trees and caves, often in colonies of over a million bats. In urban areas they roost in buildings.

Bats are distributed over temperate and tropical regions but are most abundant near the equator. Those that spend the summer in temperate regions either hibernate or migrate towards the equator in winter. Most produce only one offspring each year, so bat populations tend to recover slowly from catastrophic events.

Bats bring several benefits to humans. Their droppings contain nitrogen and phosphorus and are collected for use as fertilizer. They also help to control populations of insects that are pests of crops and carry diseases. A single bat can kill 20,000 insects in one night. In contrast, they have only a few drawbacks for humans. Some commercial fruit farmers have to use nets to protect their crops from bats, and vampire bats can transmit diseases including rabies to their animal hosts.

Humans, on the other hand, threaten the survival of bats in many ways. Some bats, such as the large flying foxes of Southeast Asia, are hunted for food. Species such as Mexican fishing bats have became locally extinct following the introduction by humans of cats and rats to their island habitats. Mining, waste disposal and irresponsible tourism threaten the caves where bats roost.

Bats have suffered grievously from the loss of their natural habitat to agriculture and forestry. A vicious cycle ensues. The decline of bats in agricultural areas causes farmers to use more chemicals to control insect pests, which risks poisoning the few remaining bats.

The endangered **lesser long-nosed bat** is one of the few bat pollinators in the southwestern USA, and is vital to the survival of agaves and giant cacti in the Sonoran Desert.

CANADA

UNITED STATES OF AMERICA

PORTUGAL

MOROCCO

BAHAMAS

CUBA

MEXICO

BELIZE JAMAICA
HONDURAS

GUATEMALA
EL SALVADOR

NICARAGUA

COSTA RICA

PANAMA

US VIRGIN
SLANDS

PUERTO
RICO

MONTSERRAT

DOMINICA

GUADELOUPE

ARUBA

NETHERLANDS ANTILLES

VENEZUELA

GUYANA

SURINAME

FRENCH GUIANA (Fr)

COLOMBIA

ECUADOR

PERU

BOLIVIA

BRAZIL

PARAGUAY

CHILE

URUGUAY

ARGENTINA

SENEGAL

GUINEA

SIERRA LEONE

LIBERIA

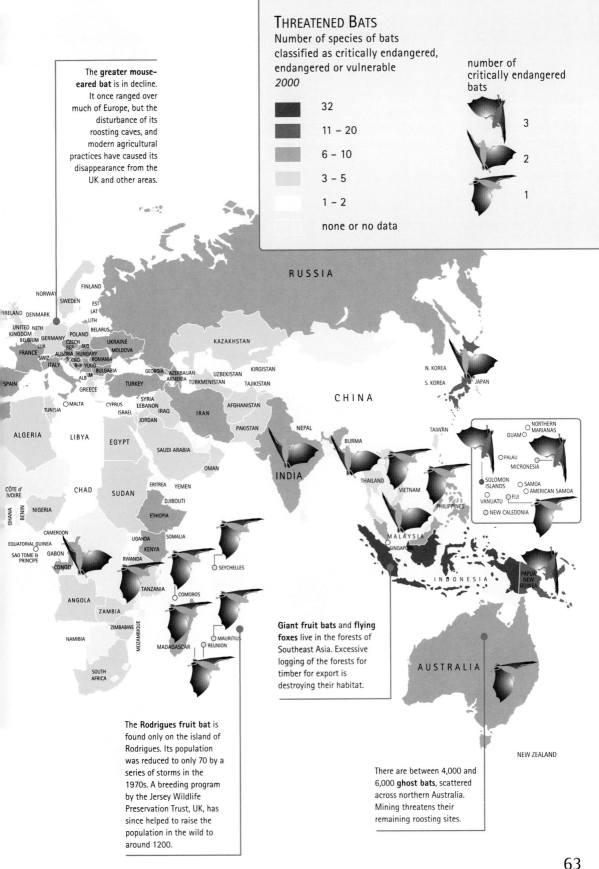

THREATENED BATS

Number of species of bats classified as critically endangered, endangered or vulnerable
2000

- 32
- 11 – 20
- 6 – 10
- 3 – 5
- 1 – 2
- none or no data

number of critically endangered bats

3

2

1

The **greater mouse-eared bat** is in decline. It once ranged over much of Europe, but the disturbance of its roosting caves, and modern agricultural practices have caused its disappearance from the UK and other areas.

NORWAY FINLAND SWEDEN EST LAT LITH IRELAND DENMARK UNITED KINGDOM NETH BELGIUM GERMANY POLAND BELARUS LUX CZECH REP S CRO SLO UKRAINE FRANCE SWIZ AUSTRIA HUNGARY MOLDOVA ITALY B-H YUGO ROMANIA ALB BULGARIA GEORGIA AZERBAIJAN UZBEKISTAN KIRGISTAN SPAIN GREECE TURKEY ARMENIA TURKMENISTAN TAJIKISTAN TUNISIA MALTA CYPRUS SYRIA LEBANON ISRAEL IRAQ IRAN AFGHANISTAN JORDAN ALGERIA LIBYA EGYPT SAUDI ARABIA PAKISTAN NEPAL OMAN CÔTE d'IVOIRE ERITREA YEMEN GHANA CHAD SUDAN DJIBOUTI BENIN NIGERIA ETHIOPIA CAMEROON UGANDA SOMALIA EQUATORIAL GUINEA GABON KENYA SAO TOME & PRINCIPE CONGO RWANDA SEYCHELLES TANZANIA COMOROS ANGOLA ZAMBIA ZIMBABWE MAURITIUS NAMIBIA MADAGASCAR REUNION SOUTH AFRICA

RUSSIA KAZAKHSTAN CHINA N. KOREA S. KOREA JAPAN TAIWAN BURMA INDIA THAILAND VIETNAM PHILIPPINES MALAYSIA SINGAPORE INDONESIA PAPUA NEW GUINEA AUSTRALIA NEW ZEALAND

NORTHERN MARIANAS GUAM PALAU MICRONESIA SOLOMON ISLANDS SAMOA AMERICAN SAMOA VANUATU FIJI NEW CALEDONIA

Giant fruit bats and **flying foxes** live in the forests of Southeast Asia. Excessive logging of the forests for timber for export is destroying their habitat.

The **Rodrigues fruit bat** is found only on the island of Rodrigues. Its population was reduced to only 70 by a series of storms in the 1970s. A breeding program by the Jersey Wildlife Preservation Trust, UK, has since helped to raise the population in the wild to around 1200.

There are between 4,000 and 6,000 **ghost bats**, scattered across northern Australia. Mining threatens their remaining roosting sites.

DOLPHINS AND WHALES

Dolphins, whales and porpoises are all classified as *Cetacea*. Some dolphins are fish, but most are aquatic mammals. The 44 species of mammalian dolphins include pilot and killer whales, and river dolphins living in South America and Asia. Dolphins usually live in groups and mainly eat fish. They are highly intelligent, and use sounds and ultrasonic pulses to communicate.

Dolphins are at risk from drowning after becoming ensnared in fishing nets. Those that live in rivers and estuaries are also adversely affected by chemical pollution and silting, and having to compete for food with humans. Their limited distribution makes them particularly vulnerable.

All whales (including the seven species of porpoise) are mammals. They must come to the water's surface to breathe through blowholes. Some whales (including the sperm, bottle-nosed, beaked and beluga) have teeth and eat fish. Others (including the gray, right, humpback and blue) strain plankton and krill from the water, using a dense fringe of blade-shaped horny plates ("baleen") in their mouths. Some whales are social, traveling in groups. They use a range of underwater sounds: barks, whistles, screams, and moans, for communication, and high-intensity clicks for navigation and to identify food sources.

Dead whales yield several products of commercial value, including meat, oil, whalebone, and ambergris which is used in perfume. Hundreds of years of whaling by increasingly effective methods has led to the near-extinction of several species, in particular the blue whale. The International Whaling Commission, set up in 1946, has attempted to combat this threat – both to whales and to the livelihood of the whalers. First it introduced quotas to give whale populations an opportunity to re-establish themselves. Then, in 1983, it introduced a temporary moratorium on commercial whaling, to take effect by 1986. Although this has not been entirely successful, it has reduced the number of whales killed, and some species, such as gray and humpback whales, are showing signs of recovery.

For some communities, whaling provides an important part of their diet, and plays a key role in their economy and culture. These are exempt

The **blue whale** is the most highly endangered whale. Since it became protected in 1967 the population has not recovered from the brink of extinction.

from the ban on commercial whaling. People from Greenland hunt fin and minke whales, those in Siberia hunt gray whales. In Alaska bowhead, and occasionally gray, whales are caught.

Whales are affected by human development, as their breeding and calving areas are often in shallow coastal waters. But tourism, in the form of "whale watching", now helps support the economies of towns and villages that once relied on income from hunting whales. It also helps to promote public understanding and appreciation of whales, which may influence governments' inclination to continue to protect them.

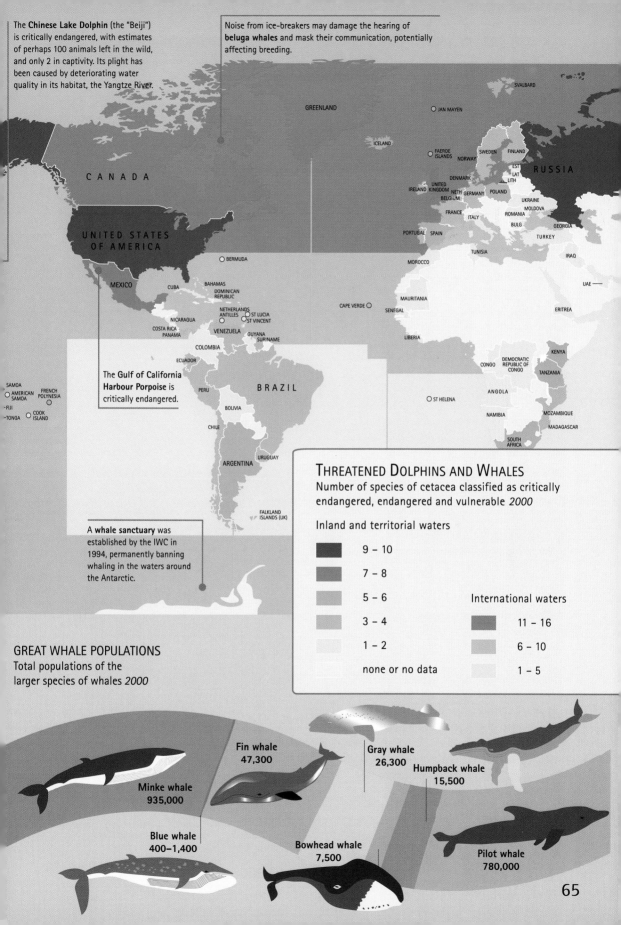

The **Chinese Lake Dolphin** (the "Beiji") is critically endangered, with estimates of perhaps 100 animals left in the wild, and only 2 in captivity. Its plight has been caused by deteriorating water quality in its habitat, the Yangtze River.

Noise from ice-breakers may damage the hearing of **beluga whales** and mask their communication, potentially affecting breeding.

The **Gulf of California Harbour Porpoise** is critically endangered.

A **whale sanctuary** was established by the IWC in 1994, permanently banning whaling in the waters around the Antarctic.

THREATENED DOLPHINS AND WHALES
Number of species of cetacea classified as critically endangered, endangered and vulnerable *2000*

Inland and territorial waters

- 9 – 10
- 7 – 8
- 5 – 6
- 3 – 4
- 1 – 2
- none or no data

International waters

- 11 – 16
- 6 – 10
- 1 – 5

GREAT WHALE POPULATIONS
Total populations of the larger species of whales *2000*

Fin whale
47,300

Gray whale
26,300

Humpback whale
15,500

Minke whale
935,000

Blue whale
400–1,400

Bowhead whale
7,500

Pilot whale
780,000

65

Reptiles are air-breathing vertebrates that have internal fertilization and scaly bodies. In evolutionary terms they are halfway between amphibians and warm-blooded vertebrates (birds and mammals). They include snakes, lizards, turtles, crocodiles and alligators.

The skins of lizards, crocodiles and snakes are used to make leather goods such as luggage, handbags and shoes. This has led to the virtual extinction of several species of crocodile and to a severe reduction in the populations of large lizards, snakes, and turtles.

Vertebrates such as frogs, toads and salamanders that are able to exploit both water and land habitats are known as amphibians (from the Greek for "living a double life"). Despite this description, however, some species are permanent land dwellers, while others are completely aquatic. Amphibians absorb oxygen through their skin, which is kept moist by mucus-secreting glands.

Frog numbers have plummeted worldwide in recent years, largely due to the spread of the fungus chytrid, which attacks keratin in their skin. It kills amphibians either by producing toxins or by stopping them from using their skins to breathe. In Australia, chytrid has helped wipe out several species of frog.

Since the early 1990s environmentally conscious Australians have been reintroducing tadpoles into ponds and streams in an attempt to bolster flagging populations but this not only spreads disease, but introduces alien genes or even alien species that displace native frogs. Exotic frog species are also being introduced accidentally, imported in crates of fruit, vegetables, and flowers.

Both reptile and amphibian populations are adversely affected by habitat loss, as a result of urbanization, agriculture or forestry. Amphibians, in particular, are susceptible to water pollution, even at low concentrations; the numbers of some amphibian species living in protected areas have declined, even though they are some distance from sources of pollution.

Deformities in frogs around the North American Great Lakes are thought to be due to pollution. Organochlorines, for example, disrupt frogs' endocrine (hormone) systems.

The **marine iguana** is only found on the Galapagos Islands and is therefore vulnerable to local pollution and the destruction of its habitat.

THREATENED AMPHIBIANS

Number of species of amphibians classified as critically endangered, endangered or vulnerable *2000*

more than 10

6 – 10

1 – 5

none or no data

a species of amphibian known to have become extinct

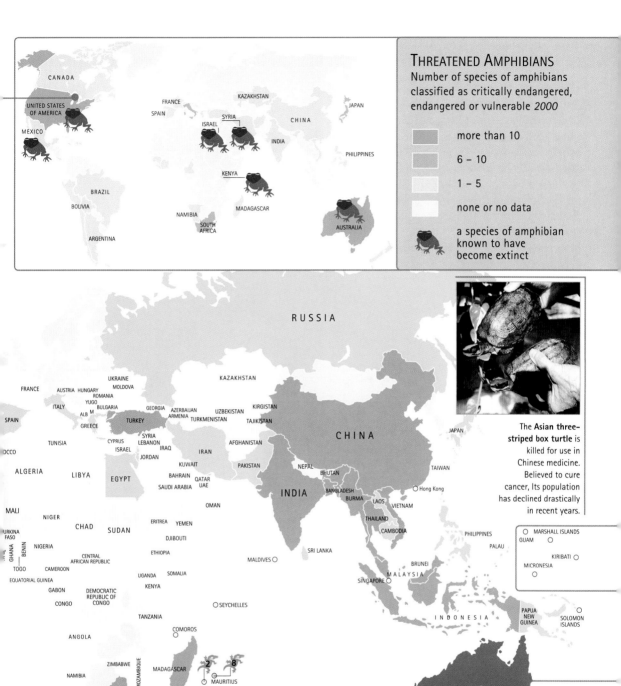

CANADA

UNITED STATES OF AMERICA

MEXICO

BRAZIL

BOLIVIA

ARGENTINA

FRANCE

SPAIN

ISRAEL SYRIA

KENYA

NAMIBIA

SOUTH AFRICA

KAZAKHSTAN

CHINA

INDIA

JAPAN

PHILIPPINES

MADAGASCAR

AUSTRALIA

RUSSIA

FRANCE AUSTRIA HUNGARY UKRAINE MOLDOVA

ITALY YUGO ROMANIA BULGARIA

ALB M GREECE GEORGIA AZERBAIJAN UZBEKISTAN KIRGISTAN

SPAIN TURKEY ARMENIA TURKMENISTAN TAJIKISTAN

TUNISIA SYRIA LEBANON IRAQ AFGHANISTAN

CYPRUS ISRAEL JORDAN IRAN PAKISTAN

OCCO ALGERIA LIBYA EGYPT KUWAIT BAHRAIN QATAR UAE SAUDI ARABIA

KAZAKHSTAN

CHINA

JAPAN

TAIWAN

NEPAL BHUTAN

INDIA BANGLADESH BURMA

Hong Kong

LAOS VIETNAM

THAILAND

MALI NIGER CHAD SUDAN ERITREA YEMEN

URKINA FASO NIGERIA DJIBOUTI CAMBODIA

GHANA BENIN CENTRAL AFRICAN REPUBLIC ETHIOPIA

TOGO CAMEROON UGANDA SOMALIA

EQUATORIAL GUINEA GABON KENYA

DEMOCRATIC REPUBLIC OF CONGO

CONGO

MALDIVES

SRI LANKA

OMAN

SINGAPORE

BRUNEI

MALAYSIA

PHILIPPINES

PALAU

MARSHALL ISLANDS

GUAM

KIRIBATI

MICRONESIA

SEYCHELLES

TANZANIA

COMOROS

ANGOLA

ZIMBABWE

NAMIBIA

MOZAMBIQUE

MADAGASCAR **2** **8**

MAURITIUS

REUNION

SOUTH AFRICA **1**

INDONESIA

PAPUA NEW GUINEA

SOLOMON ISLANDS

AUSTRALIA **1**

TUVALU

FIJI SAMOA

NEW CAL TONGA

VANUATU

COOK ISLAND

NEW ZEALAND **1**

The **Asian three-striped box turtle** is killed for use in Chinese medicine. Believed to cure cancer, Its population has declined drastically in recent years.

THREATENED REPTILES

Number of species of reptiles classified as critically endangered, endangered or vulnerable *2000*

more than 20

11 – 20

6 – 10

1 – 5

none or no data

1 number of species of reptile known to have become extinct

INVERTEBRATES

Invertebrates are animals that lack backbones. They comprise over 90 percent of animal species. Some invertebrates are soft-bodied but many have a hard outer skeleton that provides protection and anchorage for muscles; these animals are called "arthropods". The three groups of arthropods are *chelicerates* (spiders, scorpions and mites), *crustaceans* (crabs and shrimps) and *uniramians* (insects and centipedes).

The range of size and habitat of invertebrates is staggering. Some plankton measure less than two-hundredths of an inch (0.5 mm), while giant squid can grow up to 33 feet (10 metres) long. Crustaceans have been found over 2.5 miles (4 km) under the sea and spiders have been seen on Mount Everest. The practical difficulties in catching and inspecting smaller invertebrates means that the number of species can only be estimated. Some experts suggest that the number of species of insects alone is over 10 million and more are being discovered every year in remote areas of rainforest.

As new invertebrates are identified, other species are being added to the IUCN Red List. Identifying a species under threat requires money and effort. This map, together with others in the atlas, reveals a strong correlation between the number of species of invertebrates recognized as under threat in a country and the investment put into investigating them.

Invertebrates play a crucial role in many ecosystems. Other animals often rely on them for food. The plankton of the oceans support higher forms of life, including whales. Invertebrates can help in other ways too – insects pollinate flowering plants, and worms mix and aerate soil.

Some invertebrates, such as butterflies, capture the public imagination, but most are perceived of as distasteful or at least too numerous to warrant concern for their conservation. Invertebrates with restricted habitats or limited mobility are at risk both from human development and from climate change, which could, for example, eliminate a species that occurs only on a single mountain.

Monarch butterflies migrate to Mexico for the winter from places as far away as Canada. Almost all over-wintering Monarchs are concentrated in just eight groves of trees, with as many as 100,000 huddling together on a single tree for warmth. Disturbance of these groves by loggers can cause Monarchs to scatter on arrival in the autumn, jeopardizing their ability to mate the following spring.

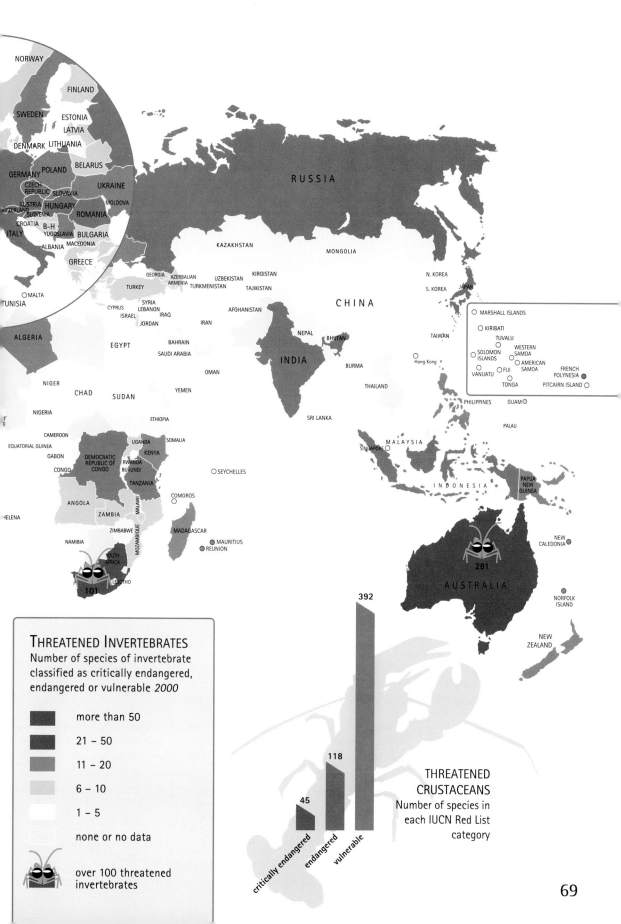

NORWAY
FINLAND
SWEDEN
ESTONIA
LATVIA
DENMARK LITHUANIA
GERMANY POLAND BELARUS
CZECH REPUBLIC SLOVAKIA UKRAINE
AUSTRIA HUNGARY MOLDOVA
SLOVENIA ROMANIA
CROATIA B-H
ITALY YUGOSLAVIA BULGARIA
ALBANIA MACEDONIA
GREECE
MALTA
TUNISIA

RUSSIA

KAZAKHSTAN
MONGOLIA

GEORGIA AZERBAIJAN UZBEKISTAN KIRGISTAN
ARMENIA TURKMENISTAN
TURKEY TAJIKISTAN
SYRIA
CYPRUS LEBANON IRAQ
ISRAEL JORDAN
AFGHANISTAN

N. KOREA
S. KOREA JAPAN

CHINA

TAIWAN

ALGERIA
EGYPT
BAHRAIN
SAUDI ARABIA
OMAN
IRAN
NEPAL BHUTAN
INDIA
BURMA
Hong Kong
THAILAND

NIGER
CHAD SUDAN YEMEN

NIGERIA
ETHIOPIA
SRI LANKA

CAMEROON
EQUATORIAL GUINEA
GABON
CONGO
DEMOCRATIC REPUBLIC OF CONGO
UGANDA SOMALIA
RWANDA KENYA
BURUNDI
TANZANIA
SEYCHELLES

ANGOLA
MALAWI
ZAMBIA
COMOROS

ZIMBABWE
NAMIBIA MOZAMBIQUE MADAGASCAR
HELENA
SOUTH AFRICA
LESOTHO
101
MAURITIUS
REUNION

PHILIPPINES GUAM
PALAU

MALAYSIA
SINGAPORE
INDONESIA
PAPUA NEW GUINEA

MARSHALL ISLANDS
KIRIBATI
TUVALU
SOLOMON ISLANDS WESTERN SAMOA
AMERICAN SAMOA
VANUATU FIJI
FRENCH POLYNESIA
TONGA
PITCAIRN ISLAND

NEW CALEDONIA

281
AUSTRALIA

NORFOLK ISLAND

NEW ZEALAND

THREATENED INVERTEBRATES
Number of species of invertebrate
classified as critically endangered,
endangered or vulnerable *2000*

- more than 50
- 21 – 50
- 11 – 20
- 6 – 10
- 1 – 5
- none or no data
- over 100 threatened invertebrates

392

118

45

critically endangered
endangered
vulnerable

THREATENED CRUSTACEANS
Number of species in
each IUCN Red List
category

69

FISH

Fish are found in rivers, lakes and oceans all over the world, and range in size from a tiny goby, half an inch (12.5 mm) in length, to the 50-foot (15-metre) whale shark. Oceanic fish range over large areas, and similar species occur around the world. Estuary and freshwater fish, however, tend to be isolated from neighbouring populations and have developed greater diversity as they adapt to their environment.

Fish congregate in schools to feed, breed and minimize the risk (to each individual) from predators. They lay eggs that hatch into larvae and develop into adult fish. Larvae and adult fish have different needs, and often live far apart. Oceanic fish may, for example, have coastal or freshwater spawning grounds.

Humans have fished the seas since prehistoric times. Most of the modern global catch comprises salt-water fish. Countries have control over fisheries in an "exclusive economic zone" up to 200 miles (320 km) from their coasts – or to the midpoint between opposing coasts. Despite this and other measures to define fishing quotas, most commercial fisheries are seriously depleted.

Freshwater fish, which represent only 6 percent of all fish caught, tend to be eaten locally, often providing crucial dietary protein in rural societies. Because freshwater species occur in limited areas, they are especially vulnerable to over-fishing and ecological damage. Dams and channels fragment habitats. Effluent and agricultural chemicals pollute them. Water abstraction sucks rivers dry.

Aquaculture (fish farming) accounts for about one-third of fish eaten around the world. Although Asia is responsible for about 90 percent of production, the industry is growing rapidly in Central and South America and in Africa. As a result, the total world fish production may rise to over 140 million tonnes by 2010.

Unregulated aquaculture can be damaging not only to the environment, but also to humans, as contaminants in fish feed are passed down the food chain. There is also the risk of exotic farmed species escaping and displacing native fish. In 1997 the World Wide Fund for Nature and

Unilever founded the Marine Stewardship Council (MSC), which established a set of principles and criteria of good fishing management. In Alaska, where overfishing had reduced salmon harvests to about 25 million fish in 1959, habitat protection has allowed stocks to recover sufficiently to enable a commercial salmon catch of 214 million fish in 1999.

Lake Victoria, the largest tropical lake in the world, used to hold over 300 species of small cichlid fish. In 1954 Nile perch were introduced to increase the size of the fishing catch. They demolished the cichlids, causing the extinction of hundreds of species. Algae, on which cichlids feed, now grow unchecked and strip oxygen from the water, jeopardizing the whole lake ecosystem.

1965	1970	1975	1980	1985	1990
50	65.3	65.7	72.2	87.1	98.5

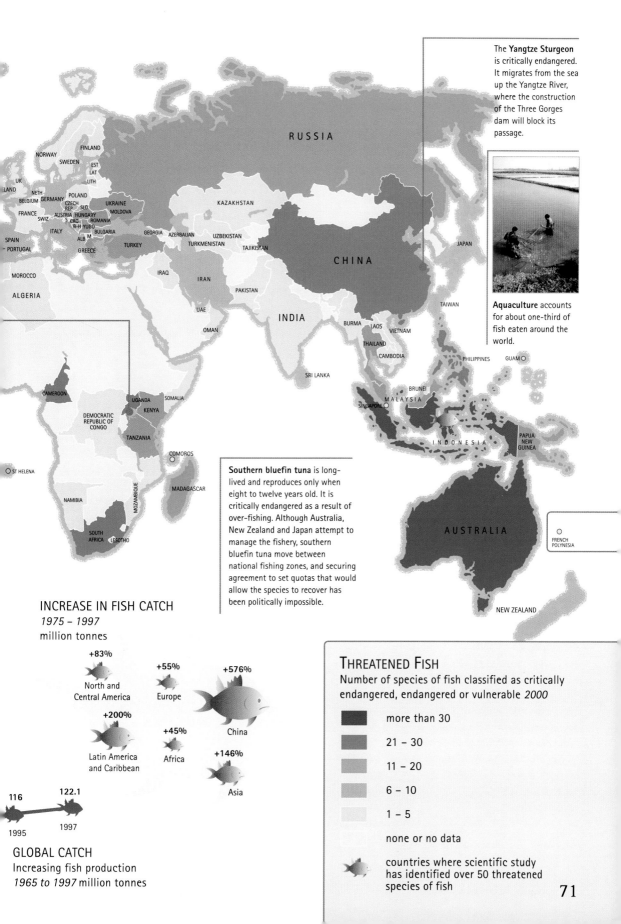

The **Yangtze Sturgeon** is critically endangered. It migrates from the sea up the Yangtze River, where the construction of the Three Gorges dam will block its passage.

Aquaculture accounts for about one-third of fish eaten around the world.

Southern bluefin tuna is long-lived and reproduces only when eight to twelve years old. It is critically endangered as a result of over-fishing. Although Australia, New Zealand and Japan attempt to manage the fishery, southern bluefin tuna move between national fishing zones, and securing agreement to set quotas that would allow the species to recover has been politically impossible.

INCREASE IN FISH CATCH
1975 – 1997
million tonnes

+83%
North and Central America

+55%
Europe

+576%
China

+200%
Latin America and Caribbean

+45%
Africa

+146%
Asia

116
1995

122.1
1997

GLOBAL CATCH
Increasing fish production
1965 to 1997 million tonnes

THREATENED FISH
Number of species of fish classified as critically endangered, endangered or vulnerable *2000*

- more than 30
- 21 – 30
- 11 – 20
- 6 – 10
- 1 – 5
- none or no data
- countries where scientific study has identified over 50 threatened species of fish

71

Plants are vital to the survival of all other life forms on earth, forming the basis of most animal food chains, including that of humans. Plants harness the sun's energy to produce their own food through the process of photosynthesis. They absorb carbon dioxide and release oxygen, helping to maintain a healthy atmosphere.

The plant kingdom is incredibly diverse, ranging from simple mosses to complex flowering plants and the 300-foot (100-meter) high redwood tree. There are between 275,000 and 300,000 species of vascular plants (ferns, conifers and flowering plants), around 34,000 of them which are threatened with extinction (see right).

Humans often carry plants and their seeds around the world, sometimes intentionally to grow for food and for decoration, sometimes inadvertently. Predators and diseases that afflict native plants are often not well adapted to attack these introduced, "exotic", plant species. As a result some exotic species become "invasive", competing with and displacing native species of plants. Exotic species may also interbreed with native plants, giving rise to hybrids. Plants endemic to a small area of land or an island are particularly at risk. Native plants on islands such as Hawaii and St. Helena, for example, have been devastated by invasive species.

Habitat destruction is an even greater threat to plant diversity. Human settlement and intensive farming continue to encroach on natural areas, threatening plants such as the Alabama canebrake pitcher-plant, which is now critically endangered following drainage of over 50 percent of the wetlands of Alabama. Unsustainable logging in forests around the world also threatens the survival of many endemic populations of plants (see pages 22-25), just as the world is waking up to the vital medicinal qualities of many species.

The **lady's slipper orchid** grows on limestone soils across the northern hemisphere. Because of its beauty it is prized by plant collectors, and has therefore always been rare. The remaining plants suffer from habitat destruction by logging and agriculture.

EXTENT OF THE THREAT
Number of species of plant in each IUCN Red List category *1997*

endangered/extinct
31

indeterminate
4,070

endangered
6,522

rare
14,505

vulnerable
7,951

total
33,418 species

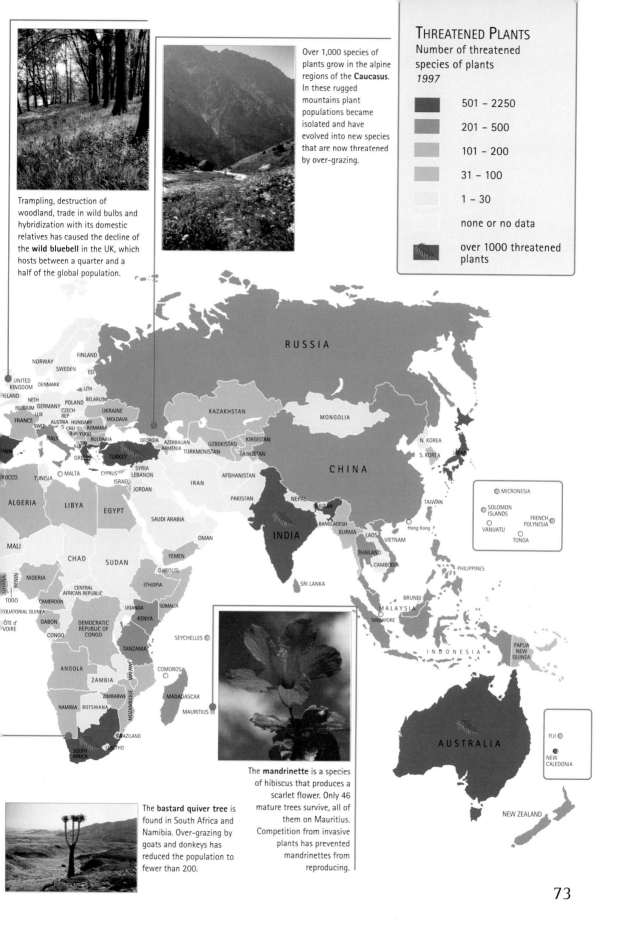

Trampling, destruction of woodland, trade in wild bulbs and hybridization with its domestic relatives has caused the decline of the **wild bluebell** in the UK, which hosts between a quarter and a half of the global population.

Over 1,000 species of plants grow in the alpine regions of the **Caucasus**. In these rugged mountains plant populations became isolated and have evolved into new species that are now threatened by over-grazing.

THREATENED PLANTS
Number of threatened species of plants
1997

- 501 – 2250
- 201 – 500
- 101 – 200
- 31 – 100
- 1 – 30
- none or no data
- over 1000 threatened plants

The **mandrinette** is a species of hibiscus that produces a scarlet flower. Only 46 mature trees survive, all of them on Mauritius. Competition from invasive plants has prevented mandrinettes from reproducing.

The **bastard quiver tree** is found in South Africa and Namibia. Over-grazing by goats and donkeys has reduced the population to fewer than 200.

73

ENDANGERED BIRDS

5

"The sedge is wither'd from the lake,
And no birds sing."

— John Keats,
"La Belle Dame Sans Merci" (1817)

BIRDS

Birds are warm-blooded vertebrates that have developed hollow bones, wings and feathers that enable most, but not all, to fly. Most birds are omnivores, eating insects, reptiles, amphibians, mammals, fish and other birds, as well as vegetable matter such as seeds.

In 2000, an estimated 12 percent, or over 1,000, of all known species of bird were considered under threat.

The greatest threat to birds is human destruction of their habitat through logging, commercial development and intensive agriculture, and the introduction of new predators, competitors and diseases. Even domestic cats, if allowed to roam free, can kill hundreds of small birds each year. Uncontrolled hunting and trapping threatens many species of birds. The imperial woodpecker, which once lived in upland forest in north eastern Mexico, was one of many species driven to extinction in the 20th century by deforestation and hunting. Migratory birds are especially vulnerable to trapping and shooting.

Intensive agriculture also threatens farmland birds, especially in North America and Europe. Winter sowing produces crops too dense for birds to nest in, and the frequent cutting of summer grass for silage destroys their nest sites. Skylark populations have decreased sharply in western Europe, but in eastern Europe, where intensive methods are not yet widespread, the bird's populations tend to be more stable.

Climate change worldwide affects the fragile balance between birds and their food supply. Plants are flowering earlier in the spring, and changes to vegetation are altering the abundance of insects, worms and other creatures. This is likely to have a significant impact on the breeding and migratory patterns of birds.

In Southeast Asia, Africa and South America deforestation is occurring at a rapid rate (see pages 42-43), and at each review more tropical rainforest birds are classified as threatened. Rainforest species, such as the Indonesian caerulean paradise-flycatcher, are most at risk from unsustainable logging and forest clearance for agriculture and exotic timber plantations.

In 1998 the **bald eagle** was officially removed from the US Fish and Wildlife Service critical list. Extensive use of pesticides had reduced its population in the USA (excluding Alaska) to fewer than 500, but conservation measures have resulted in a total of 5,000 nesting pairs.

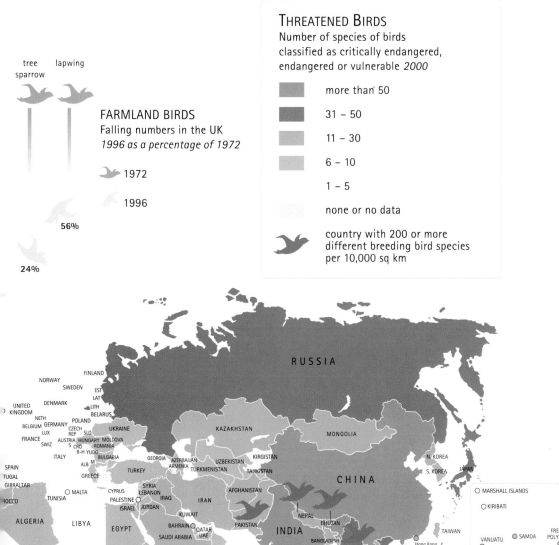

tree sparrow   lapwing

FARMLAND BIRDS
Falling numbers in the UK
1996 as a percentage of 1972

1972

1996

56%

24%

THREATENED BIRDS
Number of species of birds classified as critically endangered, endangered or vulnerable *2000*

more than 50

31 – 50

11 – 30

6 – 10

1 – 5

none or no data

country with 200 or more different breeding bird species per 10,000 sq km

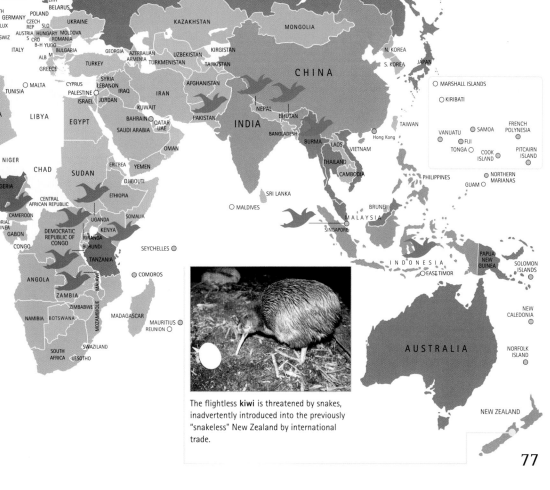

The flightless **kiwi** is threatened by snakes, inadvertently introduced into the previously "snakeless" New Zealand by international trade.

77

BIRDS OF PREY

Birds of prey include owls, and raptors such as hawks, eagles, vultures, and falcons. All birds of prey have talons for seizing their quarry, and curved beaks for tearing its flesh. They have good vision and hearing, but often a poor sense of smell. Raptors hunt during the day, and owls are nocturnal. Raptors eat other birds, mammals and carrion. Some, such as the bald eagle, can pluck fish from water. They are all skillful fliers and larger species have long, broad wings for soaring.

Many birds of prey have suffered from loss of habitat. Each breeding pair requires a large territory, which is often difficult to protect from development. Many of the chemicals used in farming are toxic to birds of prey. For example, the organochlorine pesticide DDT causes the shells of eagles' eggs to thin, making them prone to break. Prohibition of the use of such pesticides in developed countries has helped protect birds of prey, but developing countries often cannot afford the less damaging but more expensive alternatives. Birds such as the Steller's sea eagle, which feed on animals that have been shot, often suffer from lead poisoning as a result. Other birds of prey are killed for sport and food, and captured for falconry – all of which further depletes the populations of some species.

Habitat protection plays a critical role in the conservation of birds of prey. Control of poaching is important too. In many countries it is illegal to hunt birds of prey, steal their eggs or disturb their nests. Captive breeding and rehabilitation centers for injured birds can significantly help species at risk of extinction.

The **California condor** population fell below 100 in 1940 because of hunting and lead poisoning. In 1987 the remaining nine birds were captured for a breeding program at Los Angeles Zoo and at the San Diego Wild Animal Park. This has held the species back from the brink of extinction and by 2000 there were 57 reintroduced California condors living in the wild, with 98 in captivity.

CALIFORNIAN CONDOR IN CRISIS
Number of individual birds in the wild

fewer than 100

50 – 60

57

0

1940   1967   1987   2000

DECLINE OF ASIAN WHITE-BACKED VULTURE
Breeding population in Keoladeo National Park, near Bharatpur, India

UNITED STATES OF AMERICA

MEXICO

CUBA

HAITI

DOMINICAN REPUBLIC

COLOMBIA

ECUADOR

PERU

BOLIVIA

BRAZIL

PARAGUAY

URUGUAY

ARGENTINA

PORTUGAL   SPAIN

GIBRALTAR

ALGERIA

MOROCCO

WESTERN SAHARA

MAURITANIA

SENEGAL

GAMBIA

GUINEA-BISSAU

GUINEA

SIERRA LEONE

LIBERIA

FRAN

THREATENED BIRDS OF PREY

Number of species of birds of prey classified as critically endangered, endangered or vulnerable *2000*

- 7 or more
- 5 – 6
- 3 – 4
- 1 – 2
- none or no data

a critically endangered species of owl

a critically endangered species of raptor

The **Great Philippine eagle**, which produces a single chick every two years, is vulnerable to clearance of its rainforest habitat for logging and farming. No more than 300 survive, almost all on the island of Mindanao.

353 nests
1987–88

150 nests
1996–97

25 nests
1997–98

20 nests
1998–99

0 nests
1999–2000

The **white-backed** and **long-billed vultures**, once seen circling in flocks of 2,000 or more in the Indian subcontinent and Malay Peninsula, are now undergoing an alarming decline, most probably because of disease. Although it is difficult to assess their true numbers, they are reported to be extinct in some areas.

79

PARROTS AND COCKATOOS

There are over 300 species of parrot, including lorikeets, cockatoos and parakeets. As many as 95 of them, or 28 percent, are threatened – the highest proportion of any of the major bird families.

Parrots come in a variety of sizes and shapes. The pygmy parrot can be less than 3 inches (10 cm) long, while some macaws grow to over 3 feet (1 metre) in length. Most are brightly coloured. Parrots have strong, hooked beaks, which they use for breaking open nuts. Many plants, such as the oil palm, rely on parrots to disperse their seeds. A few parrots are predatory. For example, the New Zealand kea is known to attack sheep.

Most parrots live in tropical forests, nesting in tree holes. They are not built for flying long distances, which means that species are often restricted to isolated islands, making them especially vulnerable. In the West Indies at least 16 species are known to have been exterminated by European explorers, and the Puerto Rican parrot is critically endangered (see right).

Parrots, particularly the African Gray and Amazon, are excellent mimics. This ability, along with their friendly nature and lively plumage, make them popular in zoos and also as pets, with most demand coming from Europe and Japan. Some countries, such as Mexico and Australia, forbid the export of parrots in order to conserve wild populations. Despite such efforts, the legal and illegal trade in parrots is huge, threatening the viability of wild populations. Poaching alone affects 39 species and is a greater cause of mortality than natural causes.

Parrots are hunted for food, and some seed-eating parrots are hunted by farmers because they are considered to be pests. Introduced predators, such as cats, are a hazard and imported birds can displace native parrot species or introduce avian diseases.

The greatest threat to most parrot species is loss of habitat, from fire, logging and human settlement. The Species Survival Commission's conservation action plan for parrots presents techniques for their conservation in the face of habitat destruction and illegal hunting. Scarce resources in the face of competing economic interests may frustrate its effective adoption.

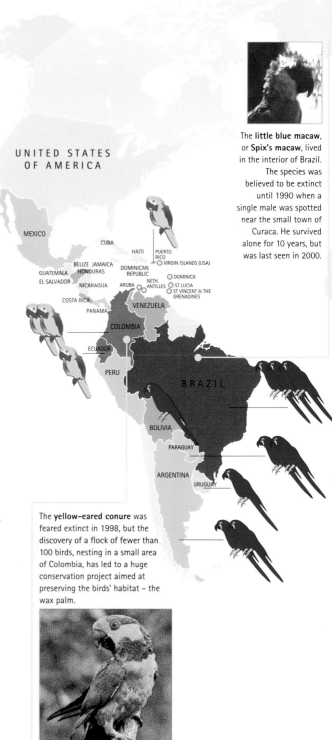

The **little blue macaw**, or **Spix's macaw**, lived in the interior of Brazil. The species was believed to be extinct until 1990 when a single male was spotted near the small town of Curaca. He survived alone for 10 years, but was last seen in 2000.

The **yellow-eared conure** was feared extinct in 1998, but the discovery of a flock of fewer than 100 birds, nesting in a small area of Colombia, has led to a huge conservation project aimed at preserving the birds' habitat – the wax palm.

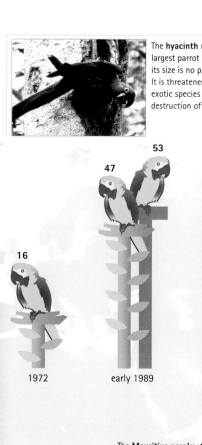

The **hyacinth macaw**, is the largest parrot in the world, but its size is no protection. It is threatened by the trade in exotic species and the destruction of its nesting habitat.

100

PUERTO RICAN AMAZON PARROT
Number of parrots

in the wild

in captivity

In September 1989 Hurricane Hugo hit Puerto Rico; only half the wild population of parrots survived.

16

47

53

53

23

40

1972

early 1989

late 1989
after Hurricane Hugo

1998

○ KIRIBATI

● PITCAIRN

○ SOLOMON ISLANDS

○ VANUATU   ● FIJI

FRENCH POLYNESIA

● NEW CALEDONIA

○ COOK ISLAND

○ NORFOLK ISLAND

Hong Kong

PHILIPPINES

The **Mauritius parakeet** is one of the most endangered parrots in the world, particularly as attempts at captive breeding have proved largely unsuccessful.

SINGAPORE ○

I N D O N E S I A

● EAST TIMOR

PAPUA NEW GUINEA

ZAMBIA

ZIMBABWE

NAMIBIA   BOTSWANA

REUNION ○   ○ MAURITIUS

AUSTRALIA

NEW ZEALAND

THREATENED PARROTS AND COCKATOOS
Number of species of parrot and cockatoo classified as critically endangered, endangered or vulnerable *2000*

	16
	11 – 15
	6 – 10
	3 – 5
	1 – 2
	none or no data

A critically endangered species of:

parrot/parakeet/conure

lorikeet

macaw

cockatoo

The flightless, nocturnal **kakapo parrot** has been reduced to a wild population of around 50 individuals. The parrots breed infrequently and are easy prey to introduced carnivorous species, such as rats. Conservation efforts have focused on relocating the remaining individuals to islands without predators and on supplementing their diet to encourage them to breed.

81

SEABIRDS

The term "seabird" is not a taxonomic classification, but simply a description of birds that live in a certain habitat, and exhibit certain physical characteristics and patterns of behavior. Many seabird species are, for example, good fliers, often exploiting prevailing winds to migrate extraordinary distances. Penguins and auks, though flightless, are strong and agile swimmers. Most seabirds catch fish and crustaceans near the ocean surface, but cormorants can dive up to 150 feet (46 metres) below the surface in search of prey. Some seabirds forage on land for insects, small rodents and rubbish. Skuas and frigatebirds harass smaller seabirds returning to land with fish, forcing their victim to drop its catch so that they can pluck it from the air before it hits the sea.

Seabirds usually nest in huge colonies, sometimes of over a million birds, on islands or cliffs where they are reasonably safe from native predatory mammals – although not always from "introduced" species. Seabirds have a low rate of reproduction, which makes them vulnerable to catastrophic events, such as oil pollution or sudden food shortages.

In the 19th century North Atlantic sailors caused the extinction of the great auk by killing whole colonies for their flesh and feathers. Seabirds are still exploited for their eggs in the Faroe Islands, Iceland, Greenland and Southeast Asia, and such "harvesting", if not properly controlled, can threaten their survival. Far out at sea, birds are still not safe from humans. Drift-nets, nicknamed "walls of death", used by large fishing boats, trap birds such as shearwaters, despite a 1992 UN moratorium on the use of nets more than 1.4 miles (2.5 km) long.

Long-line fishing also takes a huge toll of seabirds. Lines can be up to 62 miles (100 km) long, with more than 20,000 hooks. The bait on the hooks presents a ready meal for seabirds – and also the risk of becoming caught and drowned. Conservation organizations are working with the fishing industry to promote responsible fishing techniques, such as an effective bird-scarer over the fishing line, and the weighting of the line to ensure that it sinks rapidly.

Pollution is an insidious threat to seabirds. Oil-spills have contaminated Adelie Penguins in the Antarctic, and when the *Exxon Valdez* spilled 11 million gallons of crude oil into Prince William Sound in Alaska, thousands of seabirds died. Global climate change threatens all seabirds, because plankton, which are fundamental to the marine food chain, become less abundant when seawater warms.

Tuna fisheries have reported catching one seabird for every 200–300 hooks set on their long-lines. Some boats set as many as 20,000 hooks on each line.

THREATENED SEABIRDS

Number of species of seabirds classified as critically endangered, endangered or vulnerable *2000*

- 35
- 11 – 20
- 6 – 10
- 3 – 5
- 1 – 2
- none or no data

Species of seabirds classified as critically endangered

- albatross
- petrel
- booby
- shearwater
- frigate bird
- tern

The **Madeira petrel**, or Zino's Petrel, spends most of the year at sea. It nests each spring on the island of Madeira. Cats, rats and humans have reduced the population to between 250 and 400 birds.

The volcanic island of Toroshima is the main breeding site of the **short-tailed albatross**. There are only 238 breeding pairs, but this represents a recovery since its near-extinction in the 1950s. Although measures are in place to protect it from human interference, a volcanic eruption could wipe out the entire colony.

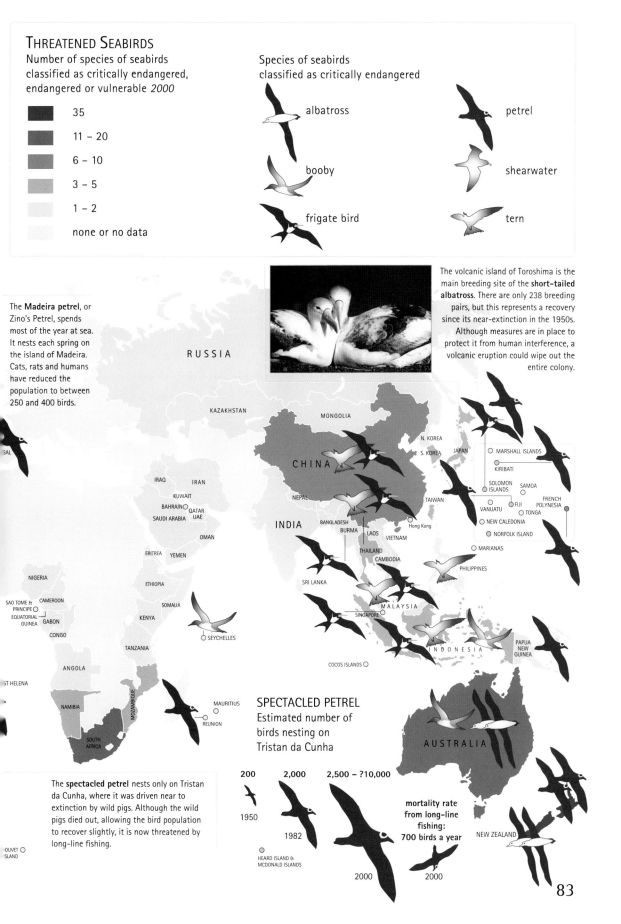

RUSSIA
KAZAKHSTAN
MONGOLIA
N. KOREA
S. KOREA
JAPAN
CHINA
IRAQ
IRAN
KUWAIT
BAHRAIN
QATAR
SAUDI ARABIA
UAE
OMAN
NEPAL
TAIWAN
INDIA
BANGLADESH
BURMA
LAOS
VIETNAM
Hong Kong
THAILAND
CAMBODIA
ERITREA
YEMEN
ETHIOPIA
SRI LANKA
PHILIPPINES
SOMALIA
NIGERIA
SAO TOME &
PRINCIPE
CAMEROON
EQUATORIAL
GUINEA
GABON
KENYA
CONGO
SEYCHELLES
MALAYSIA
SINGAPORE
TANZANIA
INDONESIA
PAPUA NEW GUINEA
ANGOLA
ST HELENA
COCOS ISLANDS
NAMIBIA
MOZAMBIQUE
MAURITIUS
REUNION
SOUTH AFRICA

○ MARSHALL ISLANDS
KIRIBATI
SOLOMON ISLANDS
SAMOA
VANUATU
FIJI
FRENCH POLYNESIA
TONGA
○ NEW CALEDONIA
○ NORFOLK ISLAND
○ MARIANAS

AUSTRALIA

SPECTACLED PETREL

Estimated number of birds nesting on Tristan da Cunha

200	2,000	2,500 – ?10,000
1950	1982	
		2000	2000

mortality rate from long-line fishing: 700 birds a year

NEW ZEALAND

HEARD ISLAND &
MCDONALD ISLANDS

OUVET
SLAND

The **spectacled petrel** nests only on Tristan da Cunha, where it was driven near to extinction by wild pigs. Although the wild pigs died out, allowing the bird population to recover slightly, it is now threatened by long-line fishing.

83

MIGRATORY BIRDS

Most migrating birds breed in the northern hemisphere in early summer, hatch their young and then head south to escape the winter. Their mobility makes them difficult to study and there is still much to be discovered about bird migration. Many projects are underway, involving ring tagging and satellite tracking. More traditional methods, relying on teams of amateur bird spotters, have been greatly helped by the ability to communicate information swiftly over the internet.

The main routes adopted by migrating birds have been identified and named, but not all birds stick to a single route. Some start on one flyway and then cross to another, and many birds take a circular tour – flying out on one route and back on another. Most migrating birds rely on stopover sites, at which they can rest, feed, and fortify themselves for the next stage of their journey. Wetlands are perhaps the most important of these habitats, but many, such as those near the Mediterranean coast, are threatened by commercial development (pages 28–29), drainage for agriculture, or, as in the case of Tunisia's Ichkeul National Park, the loss of their inflow of fresh water.

Global warming, and the resulting reduction in rainfall, may mean that birds arriving after a long flight will find their wetland feeding grounds have dried out. But rising sea levels caused by melting polar icecaps would flood coastal wetlands. In the Arctic, melting permafrost and an encroaching tree line would reduce the area of tundra on which many birds breed.

Many migrating birds never arrive at their destination. Millions are shot down, especially by farmers in the Middle East and Africa, or hunters in southern Europe, where they are killed for sport. And if they escape the bullets, they still have to negotiate built-up areas, and avoid flying into skyscrapers or becoming entangled in power cables.

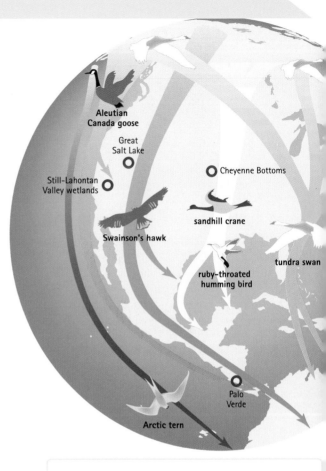

Aleutian Canada goose

Great Salt Lake

Cheyenne Bottoms

Still-Lahontan Valley wetlands

Swainson's hawk

sandhill crane

tundra swan

ruby-throated humming bird

Palo Verde

Arctic tern

MIGRATION ROUTES
Main routes taken by migrating birds to escape northern winter

Routes in Americas:
- → Pacific Flyway
- → Central Flyway
- Mississippi Flyway
- → Atlantic Flyway
- → route of the Arctic tern

Routes in Europe and Africa:
- → Iceland to northern Europe
- → Siberia to northern Europe
- → East Atlantic Flyway
- → Mediterranean/Black Sea Flyway
- → Asia–Africa Flyway
- → route of the Arctic tern

Routes in Asia and Oceania:
- → Central Asian–South Asian Flyway
- → East Asian–Australian Flyway
- → West Pacific Flyway

- O wetland site under threat selected examples

- major threat from human hunters

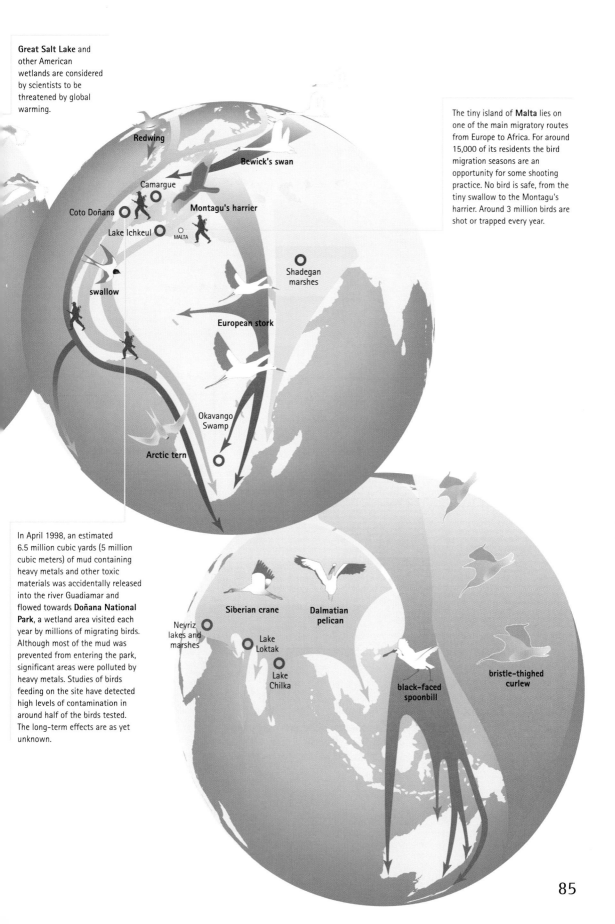

Great Salt Lake and other American wetlands are considered by scientists to be threatened by global warming.

Redwing

Bewick's swan

Camargue

Coto Doñana

Montagu's harrier

Lake Ichkeul

MALTA

Shadegan marshes

swallow

European stork

Okavango Swamp

Arctic tern

The tiny island of **Malta** lies on one of the main migratory routes from Europe to Africa. For around 15,000 of its residents the bird migration seasons are an opportunity for some shooting practice. No bird is safe, from the tiny swallow to the Montagu's harrier. Around 3 million birds are shot or trapped every year.

In April 1998, an estimated 6.5 million cubic yards (5 million cubic meters) of mud containing heavy metals and other toxic materials was accidentally released into the river Guadiamar and flowed towards **Doñana National Park**, a wetland area visited each year by millions of migrating birds. Although most of the mud was prevented from entering the park, significant areas were polluted by heavy metals. Studies of birds feeding on the site have detected high levels of contamination in around half of the birds tested. The long-term effects are as yet unknown.

Siberian crane

Dalmatian pelican

Neyriz lakes and marshes

Lake Loktak

Lake Chilka

black-faced spoonbill

bristle-thighed curlew

85

ISSUES OF CONSERVATION

"To achieve conservation results that are ecologically viable, it is necessary to conserve networks of key sites, migration corridors, and the ecological processes that maintain healthy ecosystems."

— WWF website, Endangered Spaces

There are probably about 10 million species in the kingdom of animals. About 1.2 million of them have been named and described by the scientific community, but the total number can only be estimated because much of the world has not yet been properly surveyed. New techniques are constantly being developed for examining previously uncharted regions that were thought to be barren. For example, remote-control submarines are revealing some of the remarkable species to be found in the ocean depths, and the diverse communities of bacteria, protists and fish to be found in hydro-thermal vents on the sea floor.

In lakes and oceans diversity is highest near the surface, particularly in the "photic" zone (the top 100 feet or 30 metres), where photosynthesis takes place. On land, diversity tends to be at its lowest in temperate and polar regions, possibly as a result of extinctions caused by the advance of glaciers during the recent ice-ages. In the tropics, where there is reliable moisture and warm, stable temperatures, animal diversity is much higher. Species living in these regions do not need the broad characteristics necessary for coping with varying conditions (such as drought, or winter temperatures) and adapt and diversify to suit local conditions (such as a particular type of tree, or ground cover). This leads both to a rich diversity and to a large number of endemic species. The endemic species shown on the map belong to groups that have been fairly well researched, but there are an even greater, and as yet uncounted, number of insects endemic to very small patches of land.

While the rate of extinction through natural processes is estimated as less than one species a year for every million species, habitat destruction has led to a current annual extinction rate of between 1,000 and 10,000 per million species. The disappearance of some species represents lost opportunities for exploiting genetic peculiarities that could have been harnessed for medicine and agriculture. A few will be "keystone" species, whose destruction will spell doom for entire communities.

Primates, such as the **chimpanzee**, along with other large mammals, tend to reproduce more slowly than smaller mammals, birds and reptiles. This makes them more vulnerable to natural disasters and human interference.

Isolated islands may not have a large number of species, but many will be endemic. Each of the Galapagos Islands is home to its own variation of species such as the **giant tortoise**, and the finch.

ANIMAL BIODIVERSITY
Number of mammals
per 10,000 square kilometers *2000*

- more than 1000
- 51 – 100
- 21 – 50
- 1 – 20
- none or no data

100 or more endemic species of mammal

100 or more endemic species of bird

100 or more endemic species of reptile

NORWAY
SWEDEN
FINLAND
DENMARK
ESTONIA
LATVIA
LITHUANIA
NETH
GERMANY
POLAND
BELARUS
CZECH
REPUBLIC
SLOVAKIA
UKRAINE
FRANCE
SWITZ
AUSTRIA
HUNGARY
SLOVENIA
MOLDOVA
CROATIA
ROMANIA
ITALY
B-H
YUGOSLAVIA
BULGARIA
ALBANIA
MACEDONIA
GREECE

TUNISIA
GERIA
ALGERIA
LIBYA
EGYPT

RUSSIA

KAZAKHSTAN
MONGOLIA

GEORGIA
AZERBAIJAN
ARMENIA
UZBEKISTAN
KIRGISTAN
TURKEY
TURKMENISTAN
TAJIKISTAN
SYRIA
LEBANON
IRAQ
ISRAEL
JORDAN
IRAN
AFGHANISTAN
KUWAIT
SAUDI ARABIA
UAE
OMAN

CHINA

S. KOREA
JAPAN

NEPAL
BHUTAN
PAKISTAN
BANGLADESH
BURMA
LAOS
VIETNAM
INDIA
THAILAND
CAMBODIA
SRI LANKA

MALI
NIGER
CHAD
SUDAN
ERITREA
YEMEN
BURKINA
FASO
NIGERIA
DJIBOUTI
GHANA
BENIN
CENTRAL
AFRICAN REPUBLIC
ETHIOPIA
TOGO
CAMEROON
EQUATORIAL GUINEA
SOMALIA
CÔTE d'
IVOIRE
GABON
DEMOCRATIC
REPUBLIC OF
CONGO
UGANDA
KENYA
CONGO
RWANDA
BURUNDI
TANZANIA
ANGOLA
ZAMBIA
MALAWI
MADAGASCAR
ZIMBABWE
NAMIBIA
BOTSWANA
MOZAMBIQUE
SOUTH
AFRICA
LESOTHO

SINGAPORE
MALAYSIA
INDONESIA
PHILIPPINES
PAPUA
NEW
GUINEA

SOLOMON ISLANDS
FIJI

AUSTRALIA

NEW ZEALAND

Lemurs are endemic to the island of Madagascar. They
have developed an amazing variety to fill a range of
ecological niches. **Red-ruffed lemurs** live only in the
deciduous forest of the Masoala Peninsula in northeastern
Madagascar, where logging and trapping have reduced
their numbers to between 1,000 and 10,000.

9,672
6,900
4,629
4,522

TOTAL KNOWN
SPECIES
1999

birds   reptiles   mammals   amphibians

89

PLANT BIODIVERSITY

About 300,000 species of plants have been identified, out of an estimated total of 320,000. Recently developed genetic techniques have enabled botanists to distinguish much more precisely the differences between species of plants. Flowering plants are by far the most numerous – the result of successful co-evolution with the animals that pollinate them and disperse their seeds.

Biodiversity is assessed in terms both of the number of species in a given area, and their abundance. A forest with one dominant species of tree and a handful of individuals of other tree species is considered to have a lower biodiveristy than a forest with the same number of tree species occurring in roughly equal numbers. As with animals, the diversity of plants tends to be highest near the equator, where the sun is strongest. In general, though, the lower and more widely fluctuating temperatures at high altitude, mean that diversity tends to be lower on mountains than at sea level.

Natural habitats provide numerous benefits, including the prevention of soil erosion, filtering of pollutants from water and the exchange of gases with the atmosphere. Such "ecosystem services" are not always taken into account, however, when development plans are drawn up. Over-extraction of natural resources and the cultivation of a small number of fast-growing varieties of crops condemn ever-larger areas of the Earth's surface to low biodiversity.

Plants have evolved to grow even in water of varying salinity. **Pa–Hay–Okee** ("grassy waters"), an area of 2,200 sq miles (5,700 sq km) of unique wetland habitat, was declared the Everglades National Park in 1947.

NUMBER OF PLANT SPECIES
2001

270,000 — flowering plants

12,000 — ferns

550 — conifers

145 — cycads

1,000 — club mosses

16,000 — mosses and liverworts

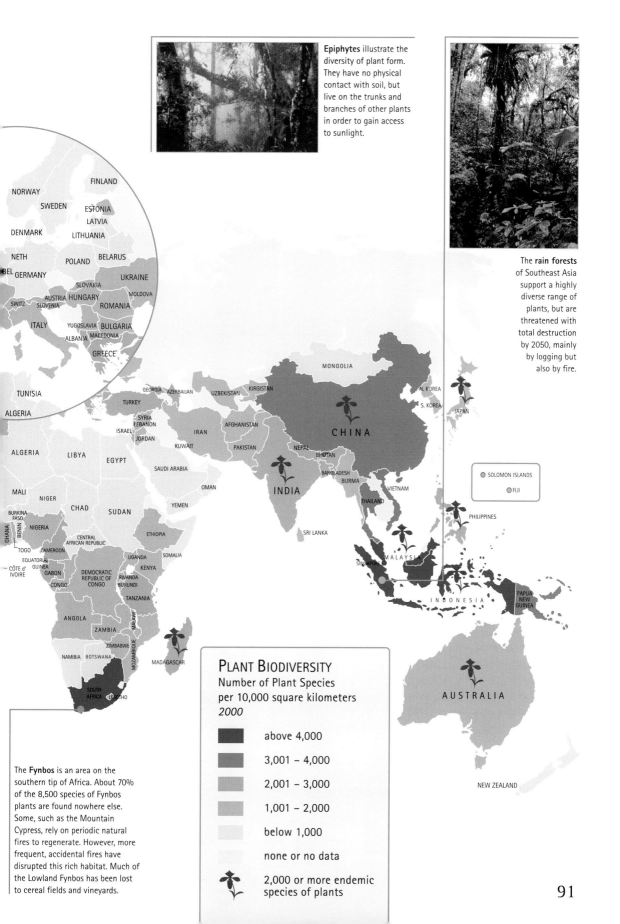

Epiphytes illustrate the diversity of plant form. They have no physical contact with soil, but live on the trunks and branches of other plants in order to gain access to sunlight.

The **rain forests** of Southeast Asia support a highly diverse range of plants, but are threatened with total destruction by 2050, mainly by logging but also by fire.

NORWAY
FINLAND
SWEDEN
ESTONIA
LATVIA
DENMARK
LITHUANIA
NETH
BELARUS
BEL
GERMANY
POLAND
UKRAINE
SLOVAKIA
AUSTRIA HUNGARY
MOLDOVA
SWITZ SLOVENIA
ROMANIA
ITALY
YUGOSLAVIA BULGARIA
ALBANIA MACEDONIA
GREECE

MONGOLIA

TUNISIA
GEORGIA AZERBAIJAN
UZBEKISTAN
KIRGISTAN
N. KOREA
ALGERIA
TURKEY
S. KOREA
JAPAN
SYRIA
LEBANON
ISRAEL
AFGHANISTAN
CHINA
JORDAN
IRAN
ALGERIA
LIBYA
KUWAIT
PAKISTAN
NEPAL
EGYPT
SAUDI ARABIA
BHUTAN
MALI
OMAN
BANGLADESH
SOLOMON ISLANDS
NIGER
YEMEN
BURMA
FIJI
CHAD
SUDAN
INDIA
VIETNAM
BURKINA
FASO
THAILAND
NIGERIA
PHILIPPINES
BENIN
ETHIOPIA
GHANA
CENTRAL
AFRICAN REPUBLIC
SRI LANKA
TOGO
CAMEROON
EQUATORIAL
UGANDA
SOMALIA
CÔTE d'
GUINEA
IVOIRE
GABON
DEMOCRATIC
REPUBLIC OF
CONGO
KENYA
RWANDA
MALAYSIA
CONGO
BURUNDI
SINGAPORE
TANZANIA
PAPUA
NEW
GUINEA
ANGOLA
INDONESIA
ZAMBIA
MALAWI
ZIMBABWE
MOZAMBIQUE
NAMIBIA BOTSWANA
MADAGASCAR

SOUTH
AFRICA LESOTHO

AUSTRALIA

NEW ZEALAND

PLANT BIODIVERSITY
Number of Plant Species
per 10,000 square kilometers
2000

- above 4,000
- 3,001 – 4,000
- 2,001 – 3,000
- 1,001 – 2,000
- below 1,000
- none or no data
- 2,000 or more endemic species of plants

The **Fynbos** is an area on the southern tip of Africa. About 70% of the 8,500 species of Fynbos plants are found nowhere else. Some, such as the Mountain Cypress, rely on periodic natural fires to regenerate. However, more frequent, accidental fires have disrupted this rich habitat. Much of the Lowland Fynbos has been lost to cereal fields and vineyards.

91

ECOLOGICAL HOTSPOTS

With threatened and degraded habitats on every continent, conservation organizations face a daunting task. They have adopted different strategies in their attempts to cope with the seemingly impossible task of counteracting the bulldozer of development.

One approach has been to target key areas. Conservation International has identified 25 priority hotspots (see map) based on three criteria: species density, the number of endemic species in the area, and the level of threat they are experiencing. Around 44 percent of all vascular plant species and 70 percent of all non-fish vertebrates can be found in the 25 hotspots, which represent about 1.4 percent of the Earth's land surface.

The WWF has taken a slightly different approach to the problem of targeting its conservation efforts. It has identified 200 ecoregions, representing 25 distinctive habitats, ranging from lush tropical rainforest to temperate forest, dry savanna to arctic tundra, deserts to wetlands, and tropical to arctic marine environments. Further targeting has resulted in the Focal 25 (see map).

Wilderness areas – where 75 percent of the natural habit is undisturbed, and there is a density of no more than 13 people per square mile (5 people per sq km) – are also the focus of the attention of conservationists. Although the size of areas such as the Amazon and Congo rain forests makes them appear unassailable, the speed of development is giving cause for deep concern. If no action is taken to protect these regions, their ecology will become degraded through fragmentation and fire damage long before the forests have vanished completely.

Ecological conservation cannot be imposed by external organizations or even by national governments. It requires the cooperation of those living and working in the area, many of whom are dependent on the very activities the conservation groups are trying to stop. So, the emphasis now is on training, education and the promotion of sustainable industries.

The **Klamath-Siskiyou** temperate forest contains 30 conifer species and 131 endemic plants, including the ancient Brewer spruce, the Port Orford cedar, and the insect-eating cobra lily.

Bering Sea

Klamath-Siskiyou Forests

California Floristic Province

Gulf of California

Chihuahuan Desert

Rivers and Streams of the American Southwest

Everglades and Florida Keys

Mesoamerica Caribbean Reef

Mesoamerica

Galapagos Islands

Caribbean

Flooded Forests of the Amazon

Brazil's Cerrado

Tropical Forests of the Northern Andes

Chocó/Darien/Western Equator

Central Chile

Atlantic Forest

Brazil's Atlantic Forest

Southwestern Amazon Rainforests

Polynesia/Micronesia

Valdivian Temperate Forest

The Atlantic forest has been reduced to around 7 percent of its original terrain, with some so fragmented as to make its survival unlikely. The **golden lion tamarin**, found nowhere else, is just one of nine critically endangered mammals in this hotspot.

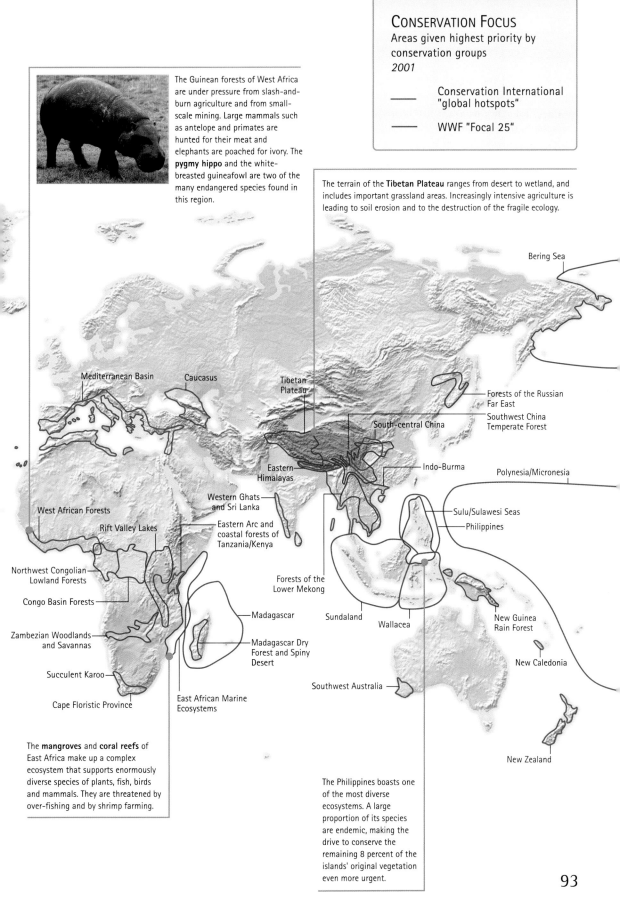

The Guinean forests of West Africa are under pressure from slash-and-burn agriculture and from small-scale mining. Large mammals such as antelope and primates are hunted for their meat and elephants are poached for ivory. The **pygmy hippo** and the white-breasted guineafowl are two of the many endangered species found in this region.

The terrain of the **Tibetan Plateau** ranges from desert to wetland, and includes important grassland areas. Increasingly intensive agriculture is leading to soil erosion and to the destruction of the fragile ecology.

Bering Sea

Mediterranean Basin

Caucasus

Tibetan Plateau

Forests of the Russian Far East

Southwest China Temperate Forest

South-central China

Indo-Burma

Polynesia/Micronesia

Eastern Himalayas

Western Ghats and Sri Lanka

Sulu/Sulawesi Seas

Philippines

West African Forests

Rift Valley Lakes

Eastern Arc and coastal forests of Tanzania/Kenya

Northwest Congolian Lowland Forests

Congo Basin Forests

Forests of the Lower Mekong

Madagascar

Sundaland

Wallacea

New Guinea Rain Forest

Zambezian Woodlands and Savannas

Madagascar Dry Forest and Spiny Desert

New Caledonia

Succulent Karoo

Southwest Australia

Cape Floristic Province

East African Marine Ecosystems

New Zealand

The **mangroves** and **coral reefs** of East Africa make up a complex ecosystem that supports enormously diverse species of plants, fish, birds and mammals. They are threatened by over-fishing and by shrimp farming.

The Philippines boasts one of the most diverse ecosystems. A large proportion of its species are endemic, making the drive to conserve the remaining 8 percent of the islands' original vegetation even more urgent.

93

CONSERVING ANIMALS

How best to save threatened animal species is a fiercely contested subject. Some believe that the only way is to preserve the natural habitats needed to support species in the wild, while others feel this is an unrealistic approach, and that captive breeding is vital to the survival of the most endangered species. The latter view is gradually winning increasing support from conservation organizations, when used in conjunction with management of populations remaining in the wild.

There are currently around 250,000 animals in the world's zoos (a fifth of them held in the UK). Many of the species most prolifically represented are not the most threatened. Zoos are expensive to run, and although some zoos receive funding from national or local governments, most rely largely on ticket sales for their income. About 600 million people visit a zoo each year, but many zoos are faced with a dilemma – whether to provide a wide range of the more popular animals in order to attract more visitors, or to concentrate on threatened species.

The predicted rate of habitat destruction could result in as many as 2,000 species needing support through captive breeding. In order to keep a population genetically diverse and healthy, populations of between 250 and 500 are necessary, with breeding between animals in different zoos. The breeding of endangered animals is in many cases managed by dedicated international programs, which keep detailed studbooks.

Conservation of animals in their natural habitat is clearly preferable, since it enables the animals to live a natural, in many cases social, existence. Sometimes animals bred in captivity can be released into the wild. This has been done with the Arabian oryx, and is being attempted with the Jamaican boa, for example. Much depends, however, on how well these released animals can be protected in the wild, and whether there is any suitable habitat left into which to release them.

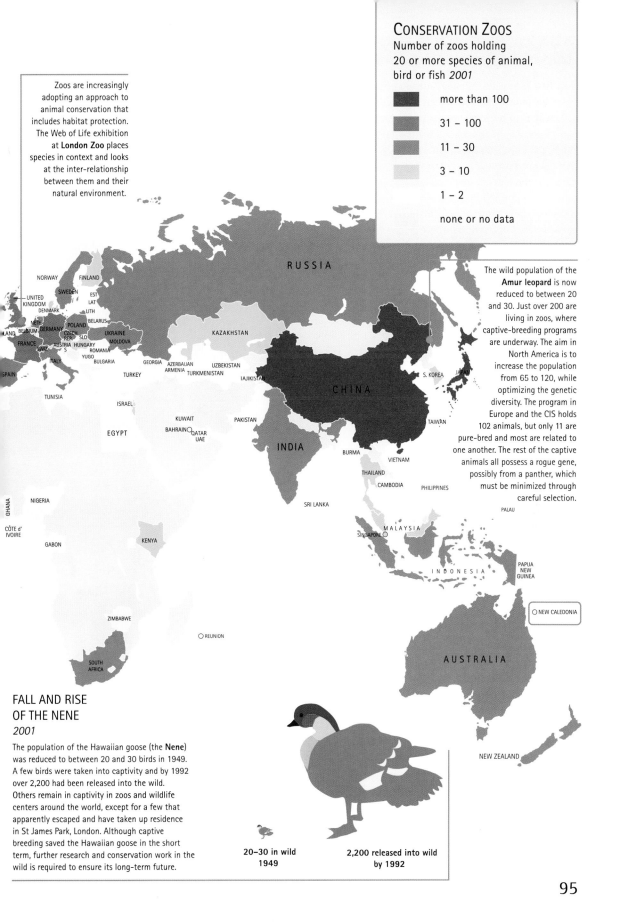

Zoos are increasingly adopting an approach to animal conservation that includes habitat protection. The Web of Life exhibition at **London Zoo** places species in context and looks at the inter-relationship between them and their natural environment.

NORWAY
FINLAND
SWEDEN
EST
UNITED
KINGDOM
LAT
DENMARK
LITH
NETH
BELARUS
GERMANY POLAND
BELGIUM
CZECH
REP
SLO
UKRAINE
FRANCE
SWIZ
AUSTRIA HUNGARY
MOLDOVA
ITALY
ROMANIA
YUGO
SPAIN
BULGARIA
GEORGIA
AZERBAIJAN UZBEKISTAN
ARMENIA TURKMENISTAN
TUNISIA
TURKEY
ISRAEL
TAJIKISTAN
KAZAKHSTAN

RUSSIA

CHINA

S. KOREA JAPAN

TAIWAN

KUWAIT
PAKISTAN
BAHRAIN QATAR
UAE
EGYPT

INDIA
BURMA
VIETNAM
THAILAND
CAMBODIA
PHILIPPINES

SRI LANKA
PALAU

GHANA
NIGERIA
CÔTE d'
IVOIRE
GABON
KENYA

MALAYSIA
SINGAPORE
INDONESIA
PAPUA
NEW
GUINEA

ZIMBABWE
REUNION
NEW CALEDONIA

SOUTH
AFRICA

AUSTRALIA

NEW ZEALAND

The wild population of the **Amur leopard** is now reduced to between 20 and 30. Just over 200 are living in zoos, where captive-breeding programs are underway. The aim in North America is to increase the population from 65 to 120, while optimizing the genetic diversity. The program in Europe and the CIS holds 102 animals, but only 11 are pure-bred and most are related to one another. The rest of the captive animals all possess a rogue gene, possibly from a panther, which must be minimized through careful selection.

FALL AND RISE OF THE NENE
2001

The population of the Hawaiian goose (the **Nene**) was reduced to between 20 and 30 birds in 1949. A few birds were taken into captivity and by 1992 over 2,200 had been released into the wild. Others remain in captivity in zoos and wildlife centers around the world, except for a few that apparently escaped and have taken up residence in St James Park, London. Although captive breeding saved the Hawaiian goose in the short term, further research and conservation work in the wild is required to ensure its long-term future.

**20–30 in wild
1949**

**2,200 released into wild
by 1992**

CONSERVING PLANTS

Botanic gardens are the zoos of the plant world. There are about 1,600 of them, containing roughly a quarter of all species of flowering plants and ferns. They are visited each year by about 150 million people worldwide and, as with zoos, public education is an important function. Some gardens incorporate herbaria, where plant specimens are dried and held to provide a permanent reference for plant diversity. Botanic gardens often also maintain seed banks. Seeds are only viable for a certain period, so drying and low-temperature storage ("cryopreservation") is used to prevent them germinating or rotting .

Governments around the world have declared nature reserves in order to protect important habitats. However, the size of a protected area is significant. Small reserves hold fewer individuals of any one plant species, which leads to a greater risk of that plant becoming extinct. Reserves need to be close to each other, or connected by similar habitat, to allow pollination and seed dispersal between them.

Preventing frequent fires is important for most plants. In the tundra the risk of fire is relatively low, plant diversity is modest and there is limited scope for agriculture. In consequence, fewer protected areas have been designated there.

Invasive plants can overwhelm ecologically balanced native flora. Physical destruction of invasive plants, pesticides and the introduction of herbivores and parasites are all used to control invasive species. Genetic pollution is a more recent hazard. Genetically modified crops could, in theory, pollinate natural relatives, with the result that genes from organisms as exotic as fish are spread to wild plants.

Eco-labelling of timber can exploit market mechanisms to promote conservation. The Forest Stewardship Council administers a certification scheme for timber extracted according to strict ecological principles. These aim either to leave forests largely intact or to give the species that are cut down an opportunity to regenerate. The success of such conservation strategies relies on harnessing the knowledge of local people about the plants around them.

Over 900 invasive species of plant, such as the **Japanese knotweed**, threaten the native flora of the USA.

96 Copyright © Myriad Editions Limited

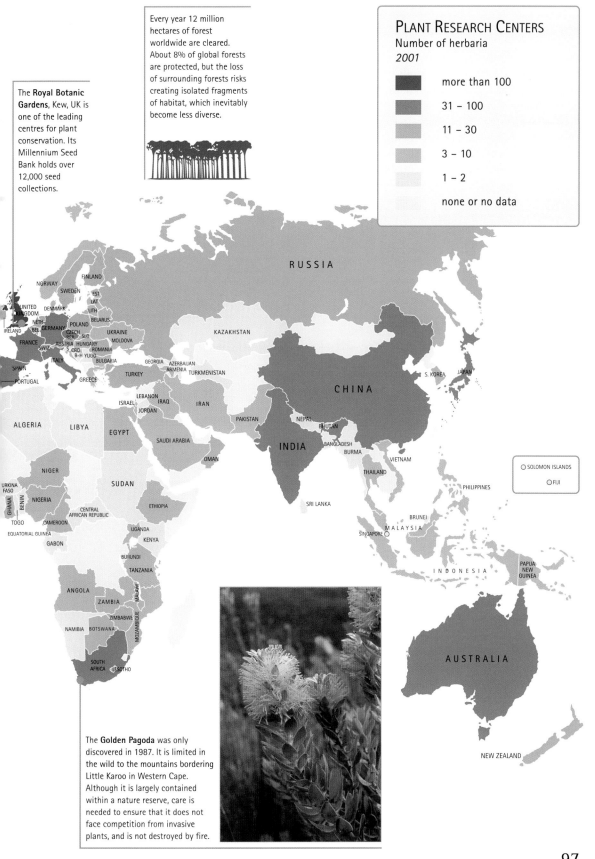

Every year 12 million hectares of forest worldwide are cleared. About 8% of global forests are protected, but the loss of surrounding forests risks creating isolated fragments of habitat, which inevitably become less diverse.

The **Royal Botanic Gardens**, Kew, UK is one of the leading centres for plant conservation. Its Millennium Seed Bank holds over 12,000 seed collections.

PLANT RESEARCH CENTERS
Number of herbaria
2001

- more than 100
- 31 – 100
- 11 – 30
- 3 – 10
- 1 – 2
- none or no data

RUSSIA

NORWAY
FINLAND
SWEDEN
EST
LAT
LITH
DENMARK
UNITED KINGDOM
IRELAND
NETH.
BEL
GERMANY
POLAND
BELARUS
CZECH REP.
SLO
UKRAINE
FRANCE
SWIZ
AUSTRIA HUNGARY
MOLDOVA
B-H YUGO
ROMANIA
CRO
ITALY
BULGARIA
SPAIN
PORTUGAL
GREECE
TURKEY
GEORGIA
AZERBAIJAN
ARMENIA
TURKMENISTAN
KAZAKHSTAN

ALGERIA
LIBYA
EGYPT
LEBANON
ISRAEL
JORDAN
IRAQ
IRAN
SAUDI ARABIA
PAKISTAN
NEPAL
BHUTAN
INDIA
BANGLADESH
BURMA
OMAN
CHINA
S. KOREA
JAPAN

NIGER
URKINA FASO
GHANA
BENIN
NIGERIA
TOGO
CAMEROON
EQUATORIAL GUINEA
GABON
SUDAN
CENTRAL AFRICAN REPUBLIC
ETHIOPIA
UGANDA
KENYA
BURUNDI
TANZANIA
VIETNAM
THAILAND
SRI LANKA
PHILIPPINES
BRUNEI
MALAYSIA
SINGAPORE

ANGOLA
ZAMBIA
MALAWI
ZIMBABWE
MOZAMBIQUE
NAMIBIA
BOTSWANA
SOUTH AFRICA
LESOTHO

INDONESIA
PAPUA NEW GUINEA

○ SOLOMON ISLANDS
○ FIJI

AUSTRALIA

NEW ZEALAND

The **Golden Pagoda** was only discovered in 1987. It is limited in the wild to the mountains bordering Little Karoo in Western Cape. Although it is largely contained within a nature reserve, care is needed to ensure that it does not face competition from invasive plants, and is not destroyed by fire.

97

CONSERVING DOMESTIC BREEDS

Humans have domesticated around 40 animal species. Over 12,000 years, thousands of different breeds have developed through selective breeding of these species as well as environmental factors. In recent decades, high-yielding breeds have been favored, with the result that other breeds are endangered or extinct. Nearly a third of domestic animal breeds are threatened by extinction. On average, two breeds are disappearing every week.

Domestic animal diversity is an important component of global biodiversity. Of the 6,500 or so breeds identified by the UN Food and Agriculture Organization (FAO), around 400 are "intensively developed": they produce high yields, but they also require a high level of maintenance, such as purpose-built shelters and specialized feed stuffs. The majority of the world's people, however, still rely on breeds that require minimum shelter and natural grazing, but do not necessarily give a high yield of milk or meat. While there is a global need to increase food production, the promotion of high-yield breeds that cannot cope with adverse local conditions is not the answer.

The preservation of a wide variety of breeds provides a genetic pool from which scientists can develop animals to meet future needs. Climate change, with its attendant impact on local environmental conditions may require the development of drought-resistant breeds. The specific genes that provide certain breeds with resistance to disease can be identified and introduced into higher-yielding breeds. As food fashions change, for health and cultural reasons, breeds can be developed to meet demand.

The FAO World Watch List assesses the viability of specific breeds within a country. Some populations have been deemed too low for survival. Others are in the "critical" or "endangered" category. This draws the attention of national organizations to threatened breeds within their borders, but it also produces anomalies. Countries in Africa, where data is not available on many breeds, register relatively few threatened breeds. On the other hand, European countries register a large number of threatened breeds because efforts are being made to conserve them.

The **angler sattelschwein** is now reduced to only 35 breeding females.

BREEDS EXTINCT OR UNDER THREAT
selected species 1999

- extinct
- critical or critical-maintained
- endangered or endangered-maintained
- not at risk
- unknown

cattle
1479 breeds

295	255
	106
	193
630	

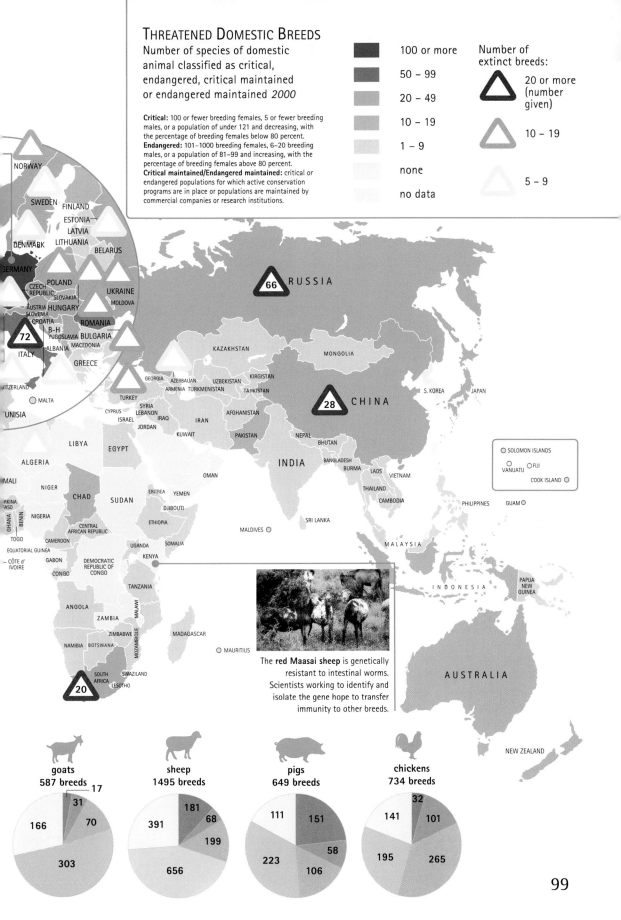

THREATENED DOMESTIC BREEDS

Number of species of domestic animal classified as critical, endangered, critical maintained or endangered maintained *2000*

■	100 or more
■	50 – 99
■	20 – 49
■	10 – 19
■	1 – 9
■	none
■	no data

Number of extinct breeds:
- △ 20 or more (number given)
- △ 10 – 19
- △ 5 – 9

Critical: 100 or fewer breeding females, 5 or fewer breeding males, or a population of under 121 and decreasing, with the percentage of breeding females below 80 percent.
Endangered: 101–1000 breeding females, 6–20 breeding males, or a population of 81–99 and increasing, with the percentage of breeding females above 80 percent.
Critical maintained/Endangered maintained: critical or endangered populations for which active conservation programs are in place or populations are maintained by commercial companies or research institutions.

The **red Maasai sheep** is genetically resistant to intestinal worms. Scientists working to identify and isolate the gene hope to transfer immunity to other breeds.

goats
587 breeds
17
31
166
70
303

sheep
1495 breeds
181
68
391
199
656

pigs
649 breeds
111
151
223
58
106

chickens
734 breeds
32
141
101
195
265

IMPORT TRADE

Industrialized countries imported over 25,700 live primates in 1997, largely for use in research laboratories. Trade in other animals, in particular parrots and reptiles, is mostly driven by the pet trade, with 235,336 parrots legally imported in 1997, a third of them into Spain. There is also a large trade in reptile skins, now fashionable for clothes and accessories. Over 200,000 alligator skins are sold each year, although many of these are from farmed, rather than wild, animals. Reptile farming practices in some countries are brutal, and include skinning snakes alive, supposedly to obtain more supple skins.

The Convention on International Trade in Endangered Species of Wild Fauna and Flora (CITES) came into force in January 1975 and currently has over 150 signatory states. Under the convention, these states agree to ban commercial international trade in some species of animal and plant and to monitor trade in others. Export and import licenses have to be issued for species covered by the convention, and trade statistics reported annually to the CITES Trade Database, managed by the World Conservation Monitoring Centre in Cambridge, UK. Compliance with the reporting requirements is by no means universal, however, with many countries failing to send in even 50 percent of the required reports.

This map (and that on pages 102–103) therefore reflects legal trade, sanctioned under CITES. It does not include the billions of dollars worth of illegal trading conducted worldwide. Nor does it indicate the mortality rate among those animals licensed for live export and import. What it does show, however, is the extent of the legal trade in species considered at risk. It also identifies the major importing countries, whose demand is driving the trade.

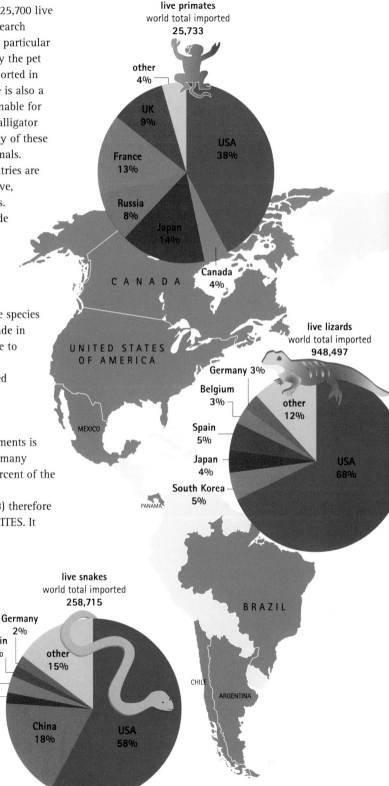

live primates
world total imported
25,733

- other 4%
- UK 9%
- France 13%
- Russia 8%
- Japan 14%
- USA 38%
- Canada 4%

live lizards
world total imported
948,497

- Germany 3%
- Belgium 3%
- other 12%
- Spain 5%
- Japan 4%
- South Korea 5%
- USA 68%

live snakes
world total imported
258,715

- Germany 2%
- Spain 2%
- France 3%
- Japan 2%
- other 15%
- China 18%
- USA 58%

CANADA

UNITED STATES OF AMERICA

MEXICO

PANAMA

BRAZIL

CHILE

ARGENTINA

live tortoises
world total imported
76,079

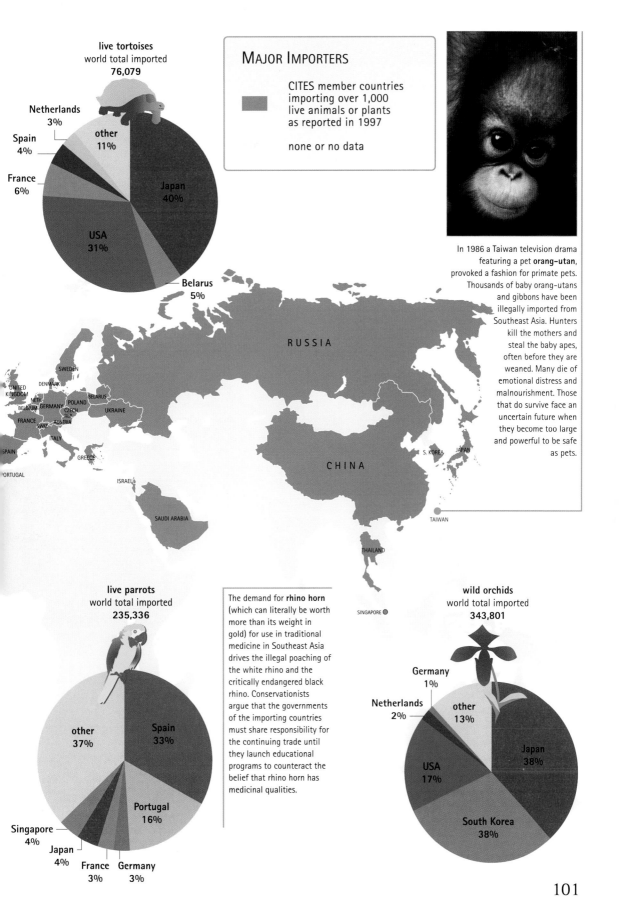

- Netherlands 3%
- Spain 4%
- France 6%
- other 11%
- Japan 40%
- USA 31%
- Belarus 5%

MAJOR IMPORTERS

CITES member countries importing over 1,000 live animals or plants as reported in 1997

none or no data

In 1986 a Taiwan television drama featuring a pet **orang–utan**, provoked a fashion for primate pets. Thousands of baby orang-utans and gibbons have been illegally imported from Southeast Asia. Hunters kill the mothers and steal the baby apes, often before they are weaned. Many die of emotional distress and malnourishment. Those that do survive face an uncertain future when they become too large and powerful to be safe as pets.

SWEDEN
DENMARK
UNITED KINGDOM
NETH.
GERMANY
BELGIUM
POLAND
BELARUS
FRANCE
CZECH REP.
AUSTRIA
SWIZ.
UKRAINE
ITALY
SPAIN
GREECE
PORTUGAL
ISRAEL
SAUDI ARABIA

RUSSIA

CHINA

S. KOREA
JAPAN

TAIWAN

THAILAND

SINGAPORE

live parrots
world total imported
235,336

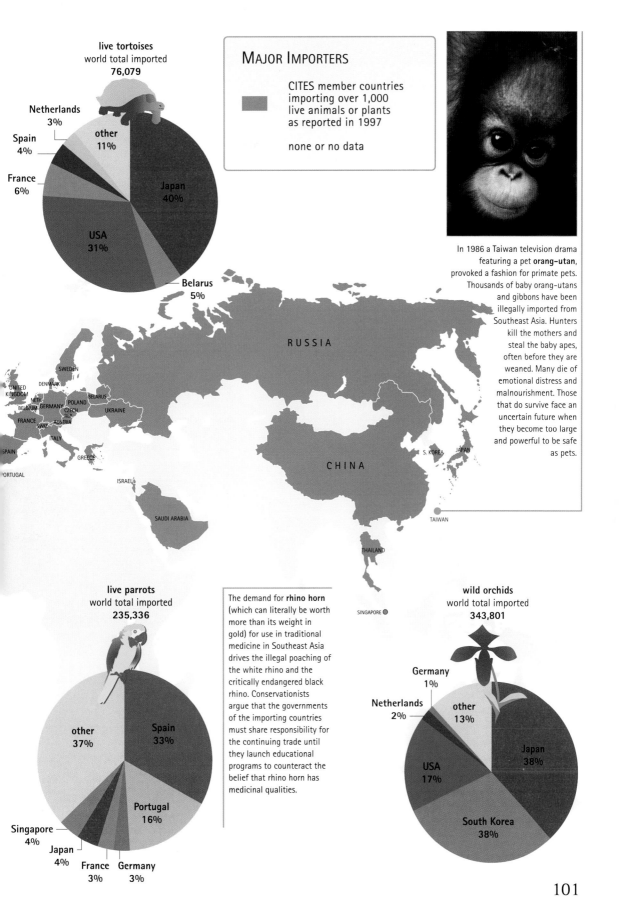

- other 37%
- Spain 33%
- Portugal 16%
- Singapore 4%
- Japan 4%
- France 3%
- Germany 3%

The demand for **rhino horn** (which can literally be worth more than its weight in gold) for use in traditional medicine in Southeast Asia drives the illegal poaching of the white rhino and the critically endangered black rhino. Conservationists argue that the governments of the importing countries must share responsibility for the continuing trade until they launch educational programs to counteract the belief that rhino horn has medicinal qualities.

wild orchids
world total imported
343,801

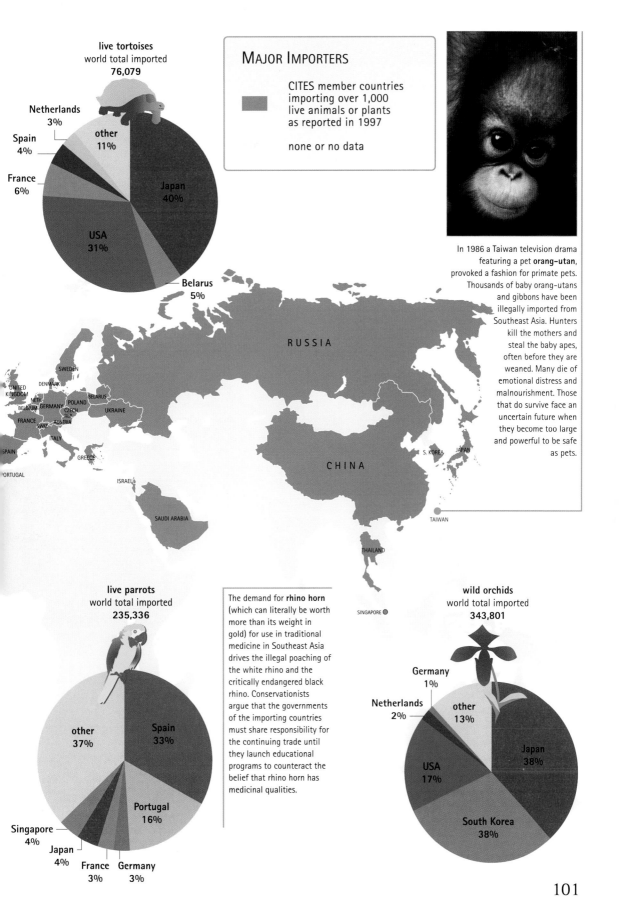

- Germany 1%
- Netherlands 2%
- other 13%
- Japan 38%
- USA 17%
- South Korea 38%

EXPORT TRADE

The financial rewards from the export of valuable wild animals and plants are considerable. Around 30,000 species are included in the Convention on International Trade in Endangered Species of Wild Fauna and Flora (CITES). For species threatened with extinction, trade is banned except in exceptional circumstances. The convention also includes species for which trade needs to be controlled in order to prevent risk of extinction. Finally, it includes species protected in at least one country, where that country has asked other CITES parties for assistance in controlling trade worldwide.

Although the Convention regularly revises the list of species it covers, it is largely the responsibility of each member state to establish the appropriate maximum number of export licenses that can be issued for a species within its territory.

Even where appropriate licensing quotas have been established, they are difficult to enforce. CITES urges countries to designate a small number of ports of exit and entry, and to train specialized enforcement officers to help identify the species being traded. Little has been done in this regard, however, although measures taken in the USA, where only nine ports are authorized to handle wildlife exports and imports, do seem to have reduced illegal trade.

The organization TRAFFIC, the trade monitoring program of WWF and IUCN–The World Conservation Union, was set up in the 1970s to assist in the implementation of CITES. In recent years it has expanded its role to look not only at trade covered by the convention but at how international sectors, including the fisheries and timber trades, impact on whole regions.

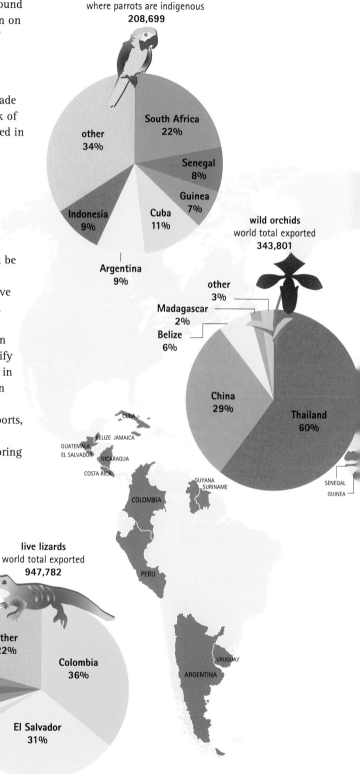

live parrots
world total exported from countries where parrots are indigenous
208,699

- South Africa 22%
- other 34%
- Senegal 8%
- Guinea 7%
- Indonesia 9%
- Cuba 11%
- Argentina 9%

wild orchids
world total exported
343,801

- other 3%
- Madagascar 2%
- Belize 6%
- China 29%
- Thailand 60%
- SENEGAL
- GUINEA

live lizards
world total exported
947,782

- Ghana 2%
- other 22%
- Colombia 36%
- Tanzania 3%
- Togo 3%
- Suriname 2%
- El Salvador 31%
- Nicaragua 2%

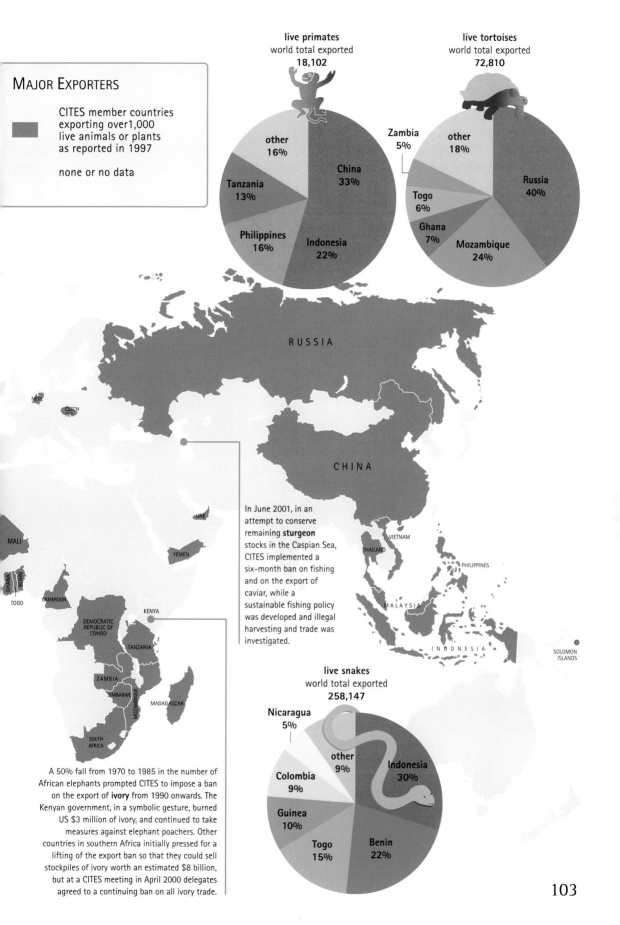

live primates
world total exported
18,102

- other 16%
- China 33%
- Tanzania 13%
- Philippines 16%
- Indonesia 22%

live tortoises
world total exported
72,810

- Zambia 5%
- other 18%
- Russia 40%
- Togo 6%
- Ghana 7%
- Mozambique 24%

MAJOR EXPORTERS

CITES member countries exporting over 1,000 live animals or plants as reported in 1997

none or no data

RUSSIA

CHINA

In June 2001, in an attempt to conserve remaining **sturgeon** stocks in the Caspian Sea, CITES implemented a six-month ban on fishing and on the export of caviar, while a sustainable fishing policy was developed and illegal harvesting and trade was investigated.

NETH.
CZECH REP.
MALI
GHANA
BENIN
TOGO
CAMEROON
DEMOCRATIC REPUBLIC OF CONGO
TANZANIA
ZAMBIA
ZIMBABWE
MOZAMBIQUE
MADAGASCAR
SOUTH AFRICA
KENYA
UAE
YEMEN
VIETNAM
THAILAND
PHILIPPINES
MALAYSIA
INDONESIA
SOLOMON ISLANDS

A 50% fall from 1970 to 1985 in the number of African elephants prompted CITES to impose a ban on the export of **ivory** from 1990 onwards. The Kenyan government, in a symbolic gesture, burned US $3 million of ivory, and continued to take measures against elephant poachers. Other countries in southern Africa initially pressed for a lifting of the export ban so that they could sell stockpiles of ivory worth an estimated $8 billion, but at a CITES meeting in April 2000 delegates agreed to a continuing ban on all ivory trade.

live snakes
world total exported
258,147

- Nicaragua 5%
- other 9%
- Indonesia 30%
- Colombia 9%
- Guinea 10%
- Togo 15%
- Benin 22%

103

"For reasons of disease, genetics and simple accident, no population of wild animals can be considered secure unless it contains around 500 individuals."

— Colin Tudge,
Last Animals at the Zoo

PROTECTED ECOSYSTEMS AND BIODIVERSITY

Countries	1 LAND AREA 000 hectares	2 TROPICAL FOREST 000 hectares	% protected	3 TEMPERATE FOREST 000 hectares	% protected	4 MANGROVES 000 hectares	% protected	5 WETLANDS 000 hectares protected
Afghanistan	65,209	0	0.0	2,076	0.0	0	0.0	–
Albania	2,740	0	0.0	1,066	1.2	0	0.0	20
Algeria	238,174	0	0.0	2,694	3.7	0	0.0	5
Angola	124,670	37,564	2.6	0	0.0	125*	0.0	–
Argentina	273,669	4,360	5.5	19,094	10.1	0	0.0	1000
Armenia	2,820	0	0.0	355	10.1	0	0.0	492
Australia	768,230	14,088	7.3	22,877	14.1	4,902	5.2	5,249
Austria	8,273	0	0.0	3,593	20.9	0	0.0	116
Azerbaijan	8,660	0	0.0	1,133	0.0	0	0.0	–
Bahamas	1,390	–	–	–	–	–	–	–
Bahrain	68	–	–	–	–	–	–	–
Bangladesh	13,017	862	3.7	0	0.0	440	8.3	596
Barbados	43	–	–	–	–	–	–	–
Belarus	20,748	0	0.0	6,280	6.5	0	0.0	19
Belgium	3,023	0	0.0	687	7.8	0	0.0	8
Belize	2,280	1,440	43.6	0	0.0	30	9.6	–
Benin	11,062	1,516	18.2	0	0.0	2*	0.0	139
Bhutan	4,700	966	22.9	1,129	37.6	0	0.0	–
Bolivia	108,438	68,638	12.1	0	0.0	0	0.0	805
Bosnia-Herzegovina	5,100	0	0.0	2,303	1.0	0	0.0	–
Botswana	56,673	12,123	19.9	0	0.0	0	0.0	6,864
Brazil	845,651	301,273	6.9	2,613	6.9	1,340	28.4	4,537
Brunei	580	–	–	–	–	–	–	–
Bulgaria	11,055	0	0.0	3,787	5.9	0	0.0	3
Burkina Faso	27,360	0	0.0	0	0.0	0	0.0	299
Burma	65,755	20,661	0.8	9,574	2.0	379*	0.0	–
Burundi	2,568	219	18.2	0	0.0	0	0.0	–
Cambodia	17,652	11,516	25.6	0	0.0	47	66.5	55
Cameroon	46,540	20,009	6.0	0	0.0	227	1.9	–
Canada	922,097	0	0.0	404,313	7.9	0	0.0	13,051
Cape Verde	–	–	–	–	–	–	–	–
Central African Rep.	62,298	17,101	20.1	0	0.0	0	0.0	–
Chad	125,920	3,516	3.6	0	0.0	0	0.0	195
Chile	74,880	0	0.0	14,526	27.1	0	0.0	100
China	932,641	109	13.0	82,710	3.9	36*	0.0	588
Colombia	103,870	53,186	10.8	0	0.0	368	22.2	400
Comoros	220	–	–	–	–	–	–	–
Congo	34,150	24,321	4.4	0	0.0	19	75.8	439
Congo, Dem. Rep.	226,705	135,071	6.6	0	0.0	22	0.0	866
Costa Rica	5,106	1,464	44.8	0	0.0	53	1.9	246
Côte-d'Ivoire	31,800	2,702	22.8	0	0.0	64*	0.0	19
Croatia	5,592	0	0.0	1,391	9.9	0	0.0	80
Cuba	10,982	1,761	15.3	0	0.0	767	7.0	–

Sources: Col 1: *World Resources 1998-1999*, Table 11.2; Col 2 & 3: *World Resources 2000-2001*, Table FG.2; Col 4: *World Resources 1998-1999*, Table 11.2 and * *World Resource 2000-2001*, Table CMI.3; Col 5: *World Resources 2000-2001*, Table BI.1

SPECIES DENSITY Number of species per million hectares					Countries
6 MAMMALS	7 BIRDS	8 REPTILES	9 AMPHIBIANS	10 PLANTS	
31	59	26	2	1,008	Afghanistan
48	162	22	9	2,139	Albania
15	32	13	2	520	Algeria
56	156	–	–	1,055	Angola
50	140	37	24	1,463	Argentina
59	169	36	5	–	Armenia
29	72	83	23	1,741	Australia
41	106	7	10	1,537	Austria
49	122	26	5	2,109	Azerbaijan
–	–	–	–	–	Bahamas
–	–	–	–	–	Bahrain
45	122	49	8	2,074	Bangladesh
–	–	–	–	–	Barbados
27	81	3	4	772	Belarus
40	125	6	12	1,073	Belgium
95	271	81	24	2,200	Belize
85	138	–	–	990	Benin
59	269	11	14	3,281	Bhutan
67	–	45	26	3,885	Bolivia
42	127	16	9	–	Bosnia-Herzegovina
43	101	41	10	563	Botswana
45	162	53	63	6,058	Brazil
–	–	–	–	–	Brunei
37	108	15	8	1,615	Bulgaria
49	112	–	–	369	Burkina Faso
62	216	51	19	1,742	Burma
76	322	–	–	1,783	Burundi
47	118	32	11	–	Cambodia
114	193	51	53	2,310	Cameroon
20	44	4	4	335	Canada
–	–	–	–	–	Cape Verde
53	137	33	12	921	Central African Rep.
27	75	1	–	322	Chad
22	71	20	12	1,269	Chile
41	114	35	30	3,340	China
75	356	124	143	10,735	Colombia
–	–	–	–	–	Comoros
62	140	–	–	1,870	Congo
74	153	62	13	1,818	Congo, Dem. Rep.
120	350	125	98	7,074	Costa Rica
73	170	–	–	1,163	Côte-d'Ivoire
43	126	16	11	–	Croatia
14	62	47	25	2,949	Cuba

PROTECTED ECOSYSTEMS AND BIODIVERSITY

Country	1 LAND AREA 000 hectares	2 TROPICAL FOREST 000 hectares	% protected	3 TEMPERATE FOREST 000 hectares	% protected	4 MANGROVES 000 hectares	% protected	5 WETLANDS 000 hectares protected
Cyprus	930	–	–	–	–	–	–	–
Czech Republic	7,728	0	0.0	2,481	27.5	0	0.0	42
Denmark	4,243	0	0.0	459	4.2	0	0.0	2,283
Djibouti	2,320	–	–	–	–	–	–	–
Dominican Republic	4,838	1,171	16.9	0	0.0	70	52.1	–
Ecuador	27,684	13,508	23.9	0	0.0	238	14.2	95
Egypt	99,545	4	0.0	134	0.0	86*	0.0	106
El Salvador	2,072	111	4.5	0	0.0	45	0.0	2
Equatorial Guinea	2,805	1,749	0.0	0	0.0	25	0.0	–
Eritrea	10,100	1	0.0	0	0.0	58*	0.0	–
Estonia	4,227	0	0.0	1,524	6.7	0	0.0	216
Ethiopia	100,000	11,937	18.8	0	0.0	0	0.0	–
Fiji	1,827	641	1.0	0	0.0	52	0.0	–
Finland	30,459	0	0.0	25,309	5.8	0	0.0	101
France	55,010	0	0.0	10,831	13.7	0	0.0	579
Gabon	25,767	21,481	3.6	0	0.0	147	3.0	1,080
Gambia	1,000	188	5.1	0	0.0	51	4.8	20
Georgia	6,970	0	0.0	3,158	0.0	0	0.0	34
Germany	34,927	0	0.0	10,401	24.8	0	0.0	673
Ghana	22,754	1,694	7.1	0	0.0	0	0.0	178
Greece	12,890	0	0.0	4,423	1.7	0	0.0	164
Guatemala	10,843	3,862	31.9	0	0.0	16	16.7	503
Guinea	24,572	3,073	1.1	0	0.0	316	0.0	225
Guinea Bissau	2,812	1,141	0.0	0	0.0	317	0.0	39
Guyana	19,685	17,844	1.3	0	0.0	159	0.0	–
Haiti	2,756	64	2.0	0	0.0	0	0.0	–
Honduras	11,189	5,273	18.3	0	0.0	231	42.2	172
Hungary	9,234	0	0.0	777	26.1	0	0.0	150
Iceland	10,025	0	0.0	–	–	–	–	59
India	297,319	44,450	8.9	9,260	8.3	304	49.6	193
Indonesia	181,157	88,744	20.9	0	0.0	2,390	32.8	243
Iran	162,200	0	0.0	2,348	12.0	21*	0.0	1,433
Iraq	43,737	–	–	–	–	–	–	–
Ireland	6,889	0	0.0	457	2.1	0	0.0	67
Israel	2,062	–	–	–	–	–	–	–
Italy	29,406	0	0.0	6,757	6.1	0	0.0	57
Jamaica	1,083	399	20.5	0	0.0	9	10.8	6
Japan	37,652	0	0.0	5,677	9.7	0.4*	0.0	84
Jordan	8,893	–	–	–	–	–	–	–
Kazakhstan	267,073	0	0.0	2,638	9.6	0	0.0	–
Kenya	56,914	3,423	8.3	0	0.0	0	0.0	49
Kirgistan	19,180	0	0.0	785	0.2	0	0.0	–
Korea (North)	12,041	0	0.0	3,967	1.1	0	0.0	–

Sources: Col 1: *World Resources 1998-1999*, Table 11.2; Col 2 & 3: *World Resources 2000-2001*, Table FG.2; Col 4: *World Resources 1998-1999*, Table 11.2 and * *World Resource 2000-2001*, Table CMI.3; Col 5: *World Resources 2000-2001*, Table BI.1

SPECIES DENSITY Number of species per million hectares					Countries
6 MAMMALS	7 BIRDS	8 REPTILES	9 AMPHIBIANS	10 PLANTS	
–	–	–	–	–	Cyprus
41	101	5	10	–	Czech Republic
27	121	3	9	895	Denmark
–	–	–	–	–	Djibouti
12	81	69	21	3,354	Dominican Republic
100	460	126	141	6,421	Ecuador
21	33	18	1	454	Egypt
106	196	57	18	2,277	El Salvador
131	194	–	–	2,312	Equatorial Guinea
50	141	38	8	–	Eritrea
40	130	3	7	1,018	Estonia
54	133	40	13	1,398	Ethiopia
3	61	20	2	1,334	Fiji
19	78	2	2	345	Finland
25	72	9	9	1,233	France
64	157	–	–	2,248	Gabon
112	269	45	29	935	Gambia
56	–	27	7	2,292	Georgia
23	73	4	6	824	Germany
78	186	–	–	1,308	Ghana
41	107	24	6	2,131	Greece
114	208	107	49	3,948	Guatemala
66	142	–	–	1,043	Guinea
71	159	–	–	655	Guinea Bissau
70	246	–	–	2,329	Guyana
2	54	77	40	3,743	Haiti
78	190	73	36	2,559	Honduras
40	98	7	8	1,155	Hungary
5	41	0	0	175	Iceland
47	137	58	31	2,363	India
81	271	91	50	5,196	Indonesia
26	60	31	2	1,489	Iran
23	49	23	2	–	Iraq
13	75	1	2	499	Ireland
91	141	76	5	2,194	Israel
29	76	13	13	1,820	Italy
23	110	35	23	3,207	Jamaica
57	75	26	18	1,679	Japan
34	68	35	–	1,069	Jordan
28	62	8	2	–	Kazakhstan
94	222	50	23	1,703	Kenya
31	–	12	1	1,412	Kirgistan
–	51	8	6	1,274	Korea (North)

PROTECTED ECOSYSTEMS AND BIODIVERSITY

Country	1 LAND AREA 000 hectares	2 TROPICAL FOREST 000 hectares	2 TROPICAL FOREST % protected	3 TEMPERATE FOREST 000 hectares	3 TEMPERATE FOREST % protected	4 MANGROVES 000 hectares	4 MANGROVES % protected	5 WETLANDS 000 hectares protected
Korea (South)	9,873	0	0.0	1,426	3.4	0	0.0	1
Kuwait	1,782	–	–	–	–	–	–	–
Laos	23,080	3,639	23.0	849	5.0	0	0.0	–
Latvia	6,205	0	0.0	1,624	10.1	0	0.0	43
Lebanon	1,023	0	0.0	36	0.0	0	0.0	1
Lesotho	3,035	89	8.7	0	0.0	0	0.0	–
Liberia	9,632	3,149	2.9	0	0.0	0	0.0	–
Libya	175,954	0	0.0	53	0.0	0	0.0	–
Lithuania	6,480	0	0.0	1,509	10.3	0	0.0	50
Luxembourg	260	0	0.0	–	–	–	–	–
Macedonia	2,543	0	0.0	1,091	9.9	0	0.0	19
Madagascar	58,154	6,940	5.5	0	0.0	310	0.2	630
Malawi	9,408	3,830	8.5	0	0.0	0	0.0	225
Malaysia	32,855	13,007	11.7	0	0.0	166	6.6	38
Maldives	–	–	–	–	–	–	–	–
Mali	122,019	6,132	2.3	0	0.0	0	0.0	162
Marshall Islands	–	–	–	–	–	–	–	–
Mauritania	102,522	–	–	–	–	–	–	–
Mauritius	203	–	–	–	–	–	–	–
Mexico	190,869	45,765	4.3	21,293	3.1	531*	0.0	1,095
Moldova	3,297	0	0.0	143	5.4	0	0.0	–
Mongolia	156,650	0	0.0	2,636	25.2	0	0.0	631
Morocco	44,630	0	0.0	1,862	2.6	0	0.0	14
Mozambique	78,409	20,863	7.5	0	0.0	565	3.7	–
Namibia	82,329	3,436	10.6	0	0.0	0	0.0	630
Nepal	14,300	1,162	18.8	2,660	20.7	0	0.0	18
Netherlands	3,392	0	0.0	235	7.4	0	0.0	325
New Zealand	26,799	0	0.0	4,212	43.8	0	0.0	39
Nicaragua	12,140	5,322	24.7	0	0.0	94	14.8	44
Niger	126,670	27	15.6	0	0.0	0	0.0	220
Nigeria	91,077	11,634	7.4	0	0.0	1,145	0.0	–
Norway	30,683	0	0.0	8,139	2.0	0	0.0	70
Oman	21,246	–	–	–	–	2*	–	–
Pakistan	77,088	807	0.6	2,083	4.7	73	39.9	62
Panama	7,443	3,744	30.9	0	0.0	180	2.1	111
Papua New Guinea	45,286	35,791	10.7	0	0.0	459	23.2	595
Paraguay	39,730	9,290	2.6	2,848	4.9	0	0.0	775
Peru	128,000	75,636	5.1	0	0.0	5*	0.0	2,932
Philippines	29,817	2,402	5.2	0	0.0	161*	0.0	68
Poland	30,442	0	0.0	8,939	12.9	0	0.0	90
Portugal	9,150	0	0.0	2,661	5.6	0	0.0	66
Qatar	1,100	–	–	–	–	–	–	–
Romania	23,034	0	0.0	8,137	2.5	0	0.0	647

Sources: Col 1: *World Resources 1998-1999*, Table 11.2; Col 2 & 3: *World Resources 2000-2001*, Table FG.2; Col 4: *World Resources 1998-1999*, Table 11.2 and * *World Resource 2000-2001*, Table CMI.3; Col 5: *World Resources 2000-2001*, Table BI.1

SPECIES DENSITY Number of species per million hectares					Countries
6 MAMMALS	7 BIRDS	8 REPTILES	9 AMPHIBIANS	10 PLANTS	
23	53	12	7	1,359	Korea (South)
17	17	24	2	193	Kuwait
61	171	23	13	–	Laos
45	117	4	7	651	Latvia
56	152	41	8	2,961	Lebanon
23	40	–	–	1,103	Lesotho
87	168	28	17	993	Liberia
14	17	10	1	331	Libya
37	109	4	7	967	Lithuania
–	–	–	–	–	Luxembourg
57	154	23	10	2,563	Macedonia
37	53	95	47	2,479	Madagascar
86	230	55	31	1,665	Malawi
95	160	110	60	4,890	Malaysia
–	–	–	–	–	Maldives
28	81	3	–	355	Mali
–	–	–	–	–	Marshall Islands
13	59	–	–	239	Mauritania
–	–	–	–	–	Mauritius
86	135	123	54	4,569	Mexico
46	119	6	9	1,173	Moldova
25	80	4	1	533	Mongolia
30	60	26	3	1,049	Morocco
42	117	39	15	1,340	Mozambique
58	109	58	12	942	Namibia
75	252	41	18	2,871	Nepal
35	120	4	10	767	Netherlands
1	51	18	1	802	New Zealand
86	207	69	25	3,256	Nicaragua
27	60	–	–	238	Niger
62	135	30	24	1,059	Nigeria
17	77	2	2	544	Norway
20	39	23	–	439	Oman
36	88	41	4	1,168	Pakistan
112	376	116	84	5,088	Panama
63	184	79	63	3,257	Papua New Guinea
90	164	35	25	2,311	Paraguay
93	310	73	76	3,674	Peru
51	64	62	30	2,907	Philippines
27	72	3	6	778	Poland
30	100	14	8	2,428	Portugal
–	–	–	–	–	Qatar
29	87	9	7	1,194	Romania

PROTECTED ECOSYSTEMS AND BIODIVERSITY

Country	1 LAND AREA 000 hectares	2 TROPICAL FOREST 000 hectares	% protected	3 TEMPERATE FOREST 000 hectares	% protected	4 MANGROVES 000 hectares	% protected	5 WETLANDS 000 hectares protected
Russia	1,688,850	0	0.0	815,551	1.8	0	0.0	10,324
Rwanda	2,467	291	77.0	0	–	0	0.0	–
Samoa	–	–	–	–	–	–	–	–
Saudi Arabia	214,969	–	–	–	–	29*	–	–
Senegal	19,253	2,076	7.0	0	0.0	158	2.9	100
Seychelles	46	–	–	–	–	–	–	–
Sierra Leone	7,162	260	20.3	0	0.0	176	0.8	295
Singapore	61	–	–	–	–	0.6*	–	–
Slovakia	4,808	0	0.0	2,308	29.6	0	0.0	37
Slovenia	2,012	0	0.0	696	8.9	0	0.0	1
Solomon Islands	2,799	2,669	0.0	0	0.0	64*	0.0	–
Somalia	62,734	11,800	1.1	0	0.0	91*	0.0	–
South Africa	122,104	10,333	5.2	52	26.4	1*	0.0	493
Spain	49,944	0	0.0	14,024	10.8	0	0.0	158
Sri Lanka	6,463	1,581	27.6	0	0.0	9	9.2	6
Sudan	237,600	12,288	12.3	0	0.0	94*	0.0	–
Suriname	15,600	13,219	4.0	0	0.0	109	35.9	12
Swaziland	1,720	–	–	–	–	0	0.0	–
Sweden	41,162	0	0.0	29,364	1.6	0	0.0	383
Switzerland	3,955	0	0.0	1,309	12.6	0	0.0	7
Syria	18,378	–	–	47	0.0	–	–	–
Tajikistan	14,060	–	–	–	–	–	–	–
Tanzania	88,359	14,356	15.8	0	0.0	323	0.4	–
Thailand	51,089	16,237	31.2	361	11.3	509	5.0	<1
Togo	5,439	224	2.6	0	0.0	3*	0.0	194
Trinidad & Tobago	513	124	7.0	0	0.0	5	5.9	6
Tunisia	15,536	0	0.0	300	2.2	0	0.0	13
Turkey	76,963	0	0.0	8,390	1.2	0	0.0	159
Turkmenistan	46,993	0	0.0	216	0.7	0	0.0	–
Uganda	19,965	3,772	17.0	0	0.0	0	0.0	15
Ukraine	57,935	0	0.0	7,046	1.6	0	0.0	716
United Arab Emirates	8,360	–	–	–	–	3*	–	–
United Kingdom	24,160	0	0.0	2,303	20.7	0	0.0	664
United States of America	915,912	443	6.7	279,386	10.4	199	60.0	1,178
Uruguay	17,481	2	0.0	97	1.0	0	0.0	435
Uzbekistan	41,424	0	0.0	231	0.0	0	0.0	–
Venezuela	88,205	55,615	59.0	0	0.0	621	65.1	264
Vietnam	32,549	4,218	10.3	723	8.8	73	2.2	12
Western Sahara	26,600	–	–	–	–	–	–	–
Yemen	52,797	–	–	–	–	8*	–	–
Yugoslavia	10,200	0	0.0	3,664	3.4	0	0.0	40
Zambia	74,339	21,989	31.9	0	0.0	0	0.0	333
Zimbabwe	38,685	15,397	12.2	0	0.0	0	0.0	–

Sources: Col 1: *World Resources 1998-1999*, Table 11.2; Col 2 & 3: *World Resources 2000-2001*, Table FG.2; Col 4: *World Resources 1998-1999*, Table 11.2 and * *World Resourc* *2000-2001*, Table CMI.3; Col 5: *World Resources 2000-2001*, Table Bl.1

SPECIES DENSITY Number of species per million hectares					Countries
6 MAMMALS	7 BIRDS	8 REPTILES	9 AMPHIBIANS	10 PLANTS	
23	58	5	4	–	Russia
110	373	–	–	1,664	Rwanda
–	–	–	–	–	Samoa
13	26	14	–	345	Saudi Arabia
72	144	37	1	780	Senegal
–	–	–	–	–	Seychelles
77	243	–	–	1,091	Sierra Leone
213	295	350	60	5,713	Singapore
50	124	12	12	1,849	Slovakia
59	164	20	16	2,535	Slovenia
37	115	43	12	2,235	Solomon Islands
43	107	49	7	768	Somalia
52	122	65	22	4,797	South Africa
22	76	15	8	1,383	Spain
47	134	77	21	1,781	Sri Lanka
43	110	–	–	507	Sudan
72	240	60	38	1,997	Suriname
–	–	–	–	–	Swaziland
17	71	2	4	498	Sweden
47	121	9	11	1,898	Switzerland
24	78	–	–	1,145	Syria
35	–	18	1	–	Tajikistan
70	184	64	30	2,231	Tanzania
72	168	81	31	3,170	Thailand
110	220	–	–	1,739	Togo
125	324	87	32	2,816	Trinidad & Tobago
31	69	25	3	873	Tunisia
28	72	25	4	2,059	Turkey
29	–	23	1	–	Turkmenistan
118	290	52	17	1,891	Uganda
28	68	5	4	1,318	Ukraine
12	33	18	–	–	United Arab Emirates
17	80	3	2	565	United Kingdom
45	68	30	28	2,036	United States of America
31	92	–	–	882	Uruguay
28	–	18	1	1,369	Uzbekistan
73	302	64	55	4,752	Venezuela
67	168	59	25	3,306	Vietnam
–	–	–	–	–	Western Sahara
18	39	21	–	446	Yemen
45	104	33	10	1,896	Yugoslavia
56	145	35	16	1,141	Zambia
81	159	46	36	1,325	Zimbabwe

THREATENED SPECIES

Countries	Number of Threatened Species					
	1 PRIMATES	2 BIG CATS	3 UNGULATES	4 RODENTS	5 BATS	6 DOLPHINS AND WHALES
Afghanistan	–	4	4	1	5	–
Albania	–	–	–	–	2	–
Algeria	1	5	7	–	4	–
Angola	4	2	1	2	3	2
Argentina	2	2	6	7	2	5
Armenia	–	–	3	1	2	–
Australia	–	–	1	16	8	5
Austria	–	–	–	2	6	–
Azerbaijan	–	–	4	1	6	–
Bahamas	–	–	–	1	1	1
Bahrain	–	–	–	–	–	–
Bangladesh	4	2	3	3	–	4
Barbados	–	–	–	–	–	–
Belarus	–	–	1	–	1	–
Belgium	–	–	–	1	5	4
Belize	1	–	1	–	1	–
Benin	3	2	1	–	1	–
Bhutan	1	3	6	2	–	1
Bolivia	2	1	2	–	1	–
Bosnia-Herzegovina	–	–	–	2	7	–
Botswana	–	2	–	–	–	–
Brazil	39	–	1	13	14	4
Brunei	1	3	–	–	–	–
Bulgaria	–	–	–	4	7	2
Burkina Faso	–	2	3	–	–	–
Burma	4	2	9	6	2	3
Burundi	3	2	–	1	–	–
Cambodia	6	2	6	3	–	–
Cameroon	14	2	1	9	2	–
Canada	–	1	1	1	1	8
Cape Verde	–	–	–	–	–	3
Central African Rep.	4	2	1	2	–	–
Chad	–	2	8	1	1	–
Chile	–	2	3	4	3	4
China	11	7	18	16	2	5
Colombia	21	–	2	4	8	2
Comoros	1	–	–	–	–	–
Congo	7	1	1	3	8	1
Congo, Dem. Rep.	9	–	–	–	–	–
Costa Rica	8	–	1	2	2	1
Côte-d'Ivoire	7	1	3	–	3	–
Croatia	–	–	–	1	7	1
Cuba	–	–	–	6	2	–

Source: Data compiled by Richard Mackay from *2000 IUCN Red List of Threatened Species*, IUCN – The World Conservation Union

Number of Threatened Species						Countries
7 REPTILES	8 AMPHIBIANS	9 INVERTEBRATES	10 FISH	11 BIRDS	12 PLANTS	
1	1	1	–	11	4	Afghanistan
2	–	3	7	3	79	Albania
1	–	11	1	6	141	Algeria
5	–	6	–	15	30	Angola
5	5	11	1	39	247	Argentina
4	–	6	–	4	31	Armenia
44	26	281	37	35	2,245	Australia
3	–	41	7	3	23	Austria
4	–	6	5	8	28	Azerbaijan
14	–	1	–	4	31	Bahamas
–	–	–	–	6	–	Bahrain
13	–	–	–	23	24	Bangladesh
2	–	–	–	1	2	Barbados
–	–	6	–	3	1	Belarus
–	–	13	1	2	2	Belgium
5	–	1	4	2	57	Belize
2	–	1	–	2	4	Benin
1	–	–	–	12	23	Bhutan
4	1	1	–	27	227	Bolivia
–	1	6	6	3	64	Bosnia-Herzegovina
–	–	–	–	7	7	Botswana
15	5	34	10	113	1,358	Brazil
5	–	–	2	15	25	Brunei
2	–	7	8	10	106	Bulgaria
1	–	–	–	2	–	Burkina Faso
–	–	2	1	35	32	Burma
–	–	3	–	7	–	Burundi
9	–	–	5	19	5	Cambodia
3	1	4	26	15	89	Cameroon
3	1	11	13	8	278	Canada
3	–	–	1	2	1	Cape Verde
1	–	–	–	3	1	Central African Rep.
1	–	1	–	5	12	Chad
1	3	–	4	21	329	Chile
17	1	4	28	73	312	China
15	–	–	5	77	712	Colombia
2	–	4	1	9	4	Comoros
2	–	1	–	4	3	Congo
–	–	45	–	28	78	Congo, Dem. Rep.
7	1	9	–	13	527	Costa Rica
4	1	1	–	12	94	Côte-d'Ivoire
–	1	8	20	4	6	Croatia
8	–	3	4	18	888	Cuba

115

THREATENED SPECIES

Countries	Number of Threatened Species					
	1 PRIMATES	2 BIG CATS	3 UNGULATES	4 RODENTS	5 BATS	6 DOLPHINS AND WHALES
Cyprus	–	–	2	–	1	–
Czech Republic	–	–	–	2	5	–
Denmark	–	–	–	–	2	–
Djibouti	–	–	4	–	1	–
Dominican Republic	–	–	–	1	–	1
Ecuador	8	–	3	73	8	4
Egypt	–	3	5	3	4	–
El Salvador	–	–	–	–	2	–
Equatorial Guinea	18	–	–	1	1	–
Eritrea	–	2	4	–	2	1
Estonia	–	–	–	1	1	1
Ethiopia	–	2	11	5	7	–
Fiji	–	–	–	–	4	1
Finland	–	–	–	1	1	3
France	–	–	1	1	8	4
Gabon	9	1	–	1	1	–
Gambia	2	1	1	–	–	–
Georgia	–	–	4	1	6	2
Germany	–	–	–	2	5	4
Ghana	6	1	1	2	2	–
Greece	–	–	1	4	5	–
Guatemala	2	–	–	1	2	–
Guinea	5	1	–	–	2	–
Guinea Bissau	3	1	2	–	–	–
Guyana	–	–	–	1	–	1
Haiti	–	–	–	2	–	–
Honduras	–	–	1	1	2	–
Hungary	–	–	–	2	7	–
Iceland	–	–	–	–	–	6
India	9	5	19	16	10	7
Indonesia	15	6	8	46	32	5
Iran	–	5	3	5	8	–
Iraq	–	2	2	1	4	2
Ireland	–	–	–	–	1	3
Israel	–	2	6	3	5	–
Italy	–	–	2	1	7	2
Jamaica	–	–	–	1	3	–
Japan	2	1	1	5	12	8
Jordan	–	1	3	–	3	–
Kazakhstan	–	3	4	5	4	–
Kenya	2	2	5	11	6	5
Kirgistan	–	3	2	2	1	–
Korea (North)	–	2	2	–	1	–

 Source: Data compiled by Richard Mackay from *2000 IUCN Red List of Threatened Species*, IUCN – The World Conservation Union

		Number of Threatened Species				Countries
7 REPTILES	8 AMPHIBIANS	9 INVERTEBRATES	10 FISH	11 BIRDS	12 PLANTS	
5	–	1	–	3	51	Cyprus
–	–	17	6	2	–	Czech Republic
–	–	10	–	1	2	Denmark
2	–	–	–	5	2	Djibouti
11	1	2	–	15	–	Dominican Republic
24	–	23	1	62	824	Ecuador
6	–	1	–	7	82	Egypt
6	–	1	–	–	42	El Salvador
2	1	2	–	5	11	Equatorial Guinea
–	–	–	–	7	–	Eritrea
3	–	3	1	3	2	Estonia
1	–	4	–	16	163	Ethiopia
6	1	2	–	12	74	Fiji
–	–	8	1	3	6	Finland
5	2	61	3	5	195	France
3	–	1	–	6	91	Gabon
1	–	–	–	2	1	Gambia
8	–	9	3	3	29	Georgia
–	–	29	7	5	4	Germany
4	–	–	–	8	103	Ghana
7	1	9	16	7	571	Greece
9	–	8	–	6	355	Guatemala
2	1	3	–	10	39	Guinea
3	–	1	–	–	–	Guinea Bissau
8	–	1	–	2	152	Guyana
8	1	2	–	14	100	Haiti
7	–	2	11	5	96	Honduras
3	–	26	–	8	30	Hungary
–	–	–	–	–	1	Iceland
16	3	22	4	70	1,236	India
19	–	29	60	113	264	Indonesia
8	2	3	7	13	2	Iran
2	–	2	2	11	–	Iraq
–	–	2	1	1	1	Ireland
6	1	10	–	12	32	Israel
7	6	41	9	5	311	Italy
8	4	5	–	12	744	Jamaica
8	10	45	7	34	707	Japan
1	–	3	–	8	9	Jordan
1	1	4	5	15	71	Kazakhstan
5	1	15	20	24	240	Kenya
1	–	3	–	4	34	Kirgistan
–	–	1	–	19	4	Korea (North)

THREATENED SPECIES

Countries	Number of Threatened Species					
	1 PRIMATES	2 BIG CATS	3 UNGULATES	4 RODENTS	5 BATS	6 DOLPHINS AND WHALES
Korea (South)	–	1	2	–	1	–
Kuwait		1	1	–	–	–
Laos	8	2	8	3	–	–
Latvia	–	–	–	1	2	–
Lebanon	–	–	–	–	5	1
Lesotho	–	1	–	–	–	–
Liberia	4	–	3	–	3	1
Libya	–	2	4	3	1	–
Lithuania	–	–	1	1	2	1
Luxembourg	–	–	–	1	5	–
Macedonia	–	–	–	3	7	–
Madagascar	39	–	–	5	7	2
Malawi	–	2	–	1	–	–
Malaysia	6	4	4	8	7	3
Maldives	–	–	–	–	–	–
Mali	2	2	7	1	–	–
Marshall Islands	–	–	–	–	–	1
Mauritania	–	2	5	2	–	1
Mauritius	–	–	–	–	3	–
Mexico	2	2	2	33	14	8
Moldova	–	–	1	1	1	1
Mongolia	–	1	4	3	–	–
Morocco	1	5	4	3	6	2
Mozambique	–	2	–	3	1	3
Namibia	–	2	1	1	2	2
Nepal	1	3	11	4	1	1
Netherlands	–	–	–	1	5	4
New Zealand	–	–	1	–	2	5
Nicaragua	1	–	1	–	1	1
Niger	–	3	7	–	–	–
Nigeria	17	2	3	4	3	–
Norway	–	–	–	–	1	7
Oman	–	–	4	1	3	–
Pakistan	–	4	5	2	4	4
Panama	11	–	1	3	1	3
Papua New Guinea	–	–	–	14	20	–
Paraguay	–	–	2	1	1	–
Peru	15	1	2	6	15	3
Philippines	2	–	5	22	10	–
Poland	–	–	1	3	5	6
Portugal	–	1	–	1	8	4
Qatar	–	–	–	–	–	–
Romania	–	–	1	6	7	2

 Source: Data compiled by Richard Mackay from *2000 IUCN Red List of Threatened Species*, IUCN – The World Conservation Union

7 REPTILES	8 AMPHIBIANS	9 INVERTEBRATES	10 FISH	11 BIRDS	12 PLANTS	Countries
						Number of Threatened Species
–	–	1	–	25	60	Korea (South)
2	–	–	–	7	–	Kuwait
7	–	–	4	19	2	Laos
–	–	6	1	3	–	Latvia
3	–	1	–	7	5	Lebanon
–	–	1	1	7	21	Lesotho
3	1	2	–	11	23	Liberia
3	–	–	–	1	57	Libya
–	–	5	1	4	1	Lithuania
–	–	4	–	1	1	Luxembourg
1	–	2	4	3	–	Macedonia
18	2	14	13	27	306	Madagascar
–	–	8	–	11	61	Malawi
14	–	3	14	37	490	Malaysia
2	–	–	–	1	–	Maldives
1	–	–	–	4	15	Mali
–	–	1	–	1	–	Marshall Islands
3	–	–	–	2	3	Mauritania
9	–	32	–	9	294	Mauritius
18	3	40	86	39	1,593	Mexico
1	–	5	9	5	5	Moldova
–	–	3	–	16	–	Mongolia
2	–	7	1	9	186	Morocco
5	–	7	2	16	89	Mozambique
4	1	1	3	11	75	Namibia
5	–	1	–	26	20	Nepal
–	–	9	1	4	1	Netherlands
11	1	15	8	62	211	New Zealand
7	–	2	–	5	98	Nicaragua
1	–	1	–	3	–	Niger
4	–	1	–	9	37	Nigeria
–	–	8	1	2	12	Norway
4	–	1	3	10	30	Oman
6	–	–	1	17	14	Pakistan
7	–	2	1	16	1,302	Panama
10	–	11	13	32	92	Papua New Guinea
3	–	–	–	26	129	Paraguay
9	1	2	–	73	906	Peru
7	2	18	26	67	360	Philippines
–	–	13	2	4	27	Poland
12	1	67	9	7	269	Portugal
2	–	–	–	6	–	Qatar
3	–	21	11	8	99	Romania

THREATENED SPECIES

Countries	Number of Threatened Species					
	1 PRIMATES	2 BIG CATS	3 UNGULATES	4 RODENTS	5 BATS	6 DOLPHINS AND WHALES
Russia	–	4	7	7	7	9
Rwanda	7	1	–	3	1	––
Samoa	–	–	–	–	2	–
Saudi Arabia	–	2	3	1	3	–
Senegal	3	2	2	1	2	1
Seychelles	–	–	1	–	4	–
Sierra Leone	4	1	3	–	1	–
Singapore	1	2	–	1	1	–
Slovakia	–	–	–	2	6	–
Slovenia	–	–	–	1	7	–
Solomon Islands	–	–	–	5	14	1
Somalia	–	2	8	2	1	–
South Africa	–	2	1	5	5	5
Spain	–	1	1	1	9	6
Sri Lanka	2	1	–	3	–	4
Sudan	2	2	11	4	4	–
Suriname	–	–	–	1	3	3
Swaziland	–	2	–	1	–	–
Sweden	–	–	–	–	3	3
Switzerland	–	–	–	1	5	–
Syria	–	2	2	1	1	–
Tajikistan	–	3	3	1	1	–
Tanzania	5	2	4	5	4	5
Thailand	4	3	8	5	4	2
Togo	3	2	2	1	–	–
Trinidad & Tobago	2	–	–	–	–	–
Tunisia	–	4	6	–	4	2
Turkey	–	3	2	4	7	2
Turkmenistan	–	3	5	3	3	–
Uganda	7	2	–	5	1	–
Ukraine	–	–	1	7	6	2
United Arab Emirates	–	1	1	–	–	1
United Kingdom	–	1	1	–	3	8
United States of America	–	4	3	10	6	9
Uruguay	–	–	–	–	1	3
Uzbekistan	–	3	3	2	2	–
Venezuela	4	–	2	5	6	3
Vietnam	11	2	8	5	3	–
Western Sahara	–	3	4	–	–	–
Yemen	–	2	3	–	1	–
Yugoslavia	–	–	–	3	7	–
Zambia	–	2	–	1	3	–
Zimbabwe	–	2	–	2	4	–

 Source: Data compiled by Richard Mackay from *2000 IUCN Red List of Threatened Species*, IUCN – The World Conservation Union

Number of Threatened Species						Countries
7 REPTILES	8 AMPHIBIANS	9 INVERTEBRATES	10 FISH	11 BIRDS	12 PLANTS	
6	–	26	13	38	214	Russia
–	–	2	–	9	–	Rwanda
–	–	–	–	–	18	Samoa
2	–	1	–	15	7	Saudi Arabia
7	–	–	–	4	31	Senegal
4	4	3	–	10	78	Seychelles
3	–	4	–	10	29	Sierra Leone
1	–	1	1	7	29	Singapore
–	–	20	7	4	–	Slovakia
–	1	38	5	1	13	Slovenia
4	–	5	–	23	42	Solomon Islands
3	–	1	3	10	103	Somalia
19	9	101	27	28	2,215	South Africa
7	3	57	10	7	985	Spain
8	–	2	8	14	455	Sri Lanka
3	–	1	–	6	10	Sudan
6	–	–	–	1	103	Suriname
–	–	–	–	5	42	Swaziland
–	–	13	1	2	13	Sweden
–	1	25	4	2	30	Switzerland
4	1	3	–	8	8	Syria
1	–	2	1	7	50	Tajikistan
5	–	46	19	33	436	Tanzania
16	–	1	14	37	385	Thailand
3	–	–	–	–	4	Togo
5	–	–	–	1	21	Trinidad & Tobago
2	–	5	–	5	24	Tunisia
14	2	9	18	11	1,870	Turkey
2	–	3	5	6	17	Turkmenistan
1	–	10	28	13	15	Uganda
2	–	13	12	8	52	Ukraine
2	–	–	1	8	–	United Arab Emirates
–	–	10	1	2	18	United Kingdom
28	26	594	123	55	4,669	United States of America
–	–	1	–	11	15	Uruguay
1	–	1	3	9	41	Uzbekistan
14	–	1	5	24	46	Venezuela
12	1	–	3	35	341	Vietnam
2	–	–	–	–	–	Western Sahara
2	–	2	–	12	149	Yemen
1	–	19	13	5	155	Yugoslavia
–	–	6	–	11	12	Zambia
1	–	2	–	10	100	Zimbabwe

121

REFERENCES

Part 1 EXTINCTION IS FOREVER

12–13 EVOLUTION

C Darwin, *On the Origin of Species by Means of Natural Selection, or The Preservation of Favoured Races in the Struggle for Life*, 1859
<daphne.palomar.edu>
<www.ucmp.berkeley.edu/history/evolution.html>
<www.geocities.com/RainForest/Canopy/3220/taxonomy.html>

14–15 MASS EXTINCTIONS

<www.bbc.co.uk/education/darwin/exfiles/index.htm>
<www.wri.org/biodiv/extinct.html>

16–17 DINOSAURS

<www.enchantedlearning.com/subjects/ dinosaurs>
<library.thinkquest.org>
<www.dinosauria.com/index.html>
<www.ucmp.berkeley.edu/diapsids/dinosaur.html>

18–19 HOMINIDS

Institute of Human Origins: <www.asu.edu/clas/iho/>
<www.talkorigins.org>

Part 2 ECOSYSTEMS

22–23 TROPICAL FORESTS

Food and Agricultural Organization, *State of the World's Forests 1999*, FAO 1999
World Wide Fund for Nature, *Forests for Life*, WWF-UK 1996
Protected Tropical Forest and **Tropical Forest by Region:** *World Resources 2000–2001*, WRI 2000, Table FG.2
Tropical Forest Past and Future: D Bryant, D Nielsen, L Tangley, *The Last Frontier Forests: Ecosystems and Economics on the Edge*, WRI, 1997

24–25 TEMPERATE FORESTS

Food and Agricultural Organization, *State of the World's Forests 1999*, FAO 1999
WWF, *Forests for Life*, WWF-UK 1996
Protected Temperate Forest and **Temperate Forest by Region:** *World Resources 2000–2001*, WRI 2000, Table FG.2
Temperate Forest Past and Future: D Bryant, D Nielsen, L Tangley, *The Last Frontier Forests: Ecosystems and Economics on the Edge*, WRI, 1997

26–27 GRASSLANDS

World Resources 2000–2001, World Resources Institute, 2000 pp119–139
Sauer, J R, J E Hines, I Thomas, J Fallon, and G Gough, *The North American Breeding Bird Survey, Results and Analysis 1966–1998. Version 98.1*, USGS Patuxent Wildlife Research Center, 1999
Asian steppes: *World Resources 2000-2001*, pp212–224
Grasslands: R White, S Murray, M Rohweder, PAGE Analysis, Map 15
<www.wri.org/wr2000/grasslands_page.html>
Current Land Use: *World Resources 2000-2001*, p123

28–29 WETLANDS

Wetlands International <www.ramsar.org>
International Rivers Network <www.irn.org>
WWF <www.panda.org>
Wetlands of International Importance: *World Resources 2000-2001*, WRI, 2000, Table BI.1
Coastal Development: D Bryant, D Nielsen, L Tangley, *Coastlines at Risk*, WRI Indicator Brief, 1995

30–31 MANGROVES

<www.agri-aqua.ait.ac.th/mangroves/ECOLOGY.html>
<www.floridaplants.com/horticulture/mangrove.htm>
<ibm590.aims.gov.au/reports>
Mangroves Protected: *World Resources 1998–1999*, WRI, 1998, Table 11.2; World Resources 2000-2001, WRI, 2000, Table CMI.3
Florida Mangroves: <http://www.unep-wcmc.org/>
Mangrove loss in Thailand: < www.agri-aqua.ait.ac.th/mangroves/Costtab3.html>
Mangrove distribution:
<www.sierraclub.ca/national/shrimp/biod.html>
Total value of loss: R Costanza *et al*, "The value of the world's ecosystem services and natural capital", *Nature*, 387:253–260

32–33 CORAL REEFS

D Bryant, L Burke, J McManus, M Spalding, *Reefs at Risk*, World Resources Institute, 1998
The State of Coral: World Conservation Monitoring Centre, 1997 <www.unep-wcmc.org>
Coral Reef Destroyed: C Wilkinson, *Status of Coral Reefs of the World: 2000*, Australian Institute of Marine Science, 2000

Part 3 FRAGILE REGIONS

36–37 THE ARCTIC
C Zöckler & I Lysenko, *Water Birds on the Edge* (March 2000) World Conservation Monitoring Centre

Protected Areas: Conservation of Arctic Flora and Fauna <www.grida.no.db/maps/caff>

Red-Breasted Goose: J M Hunter & J M Black, *International Action Plan for the Red-Breasted Goose*, BirdLife International, European Commission <europa.eu.int/comm/environment/nature/directive/birdactionplan/brantaruficollis.htm>

38–39 THE ANTARCTIC
The World Factbook, 2000, Central Intelligence Agency, 2000

2000 IUCN Red List of Threatened Species, IUCN – The WorldConservation Union

Protected Areas: <www.nerc-bas.ac.uk/public/magic/protected-area/spa/spamap.html>

Southern Ocean Sanctuary: <ourworld.compuserve.com/homepages/iwcoffice/Catches.htm>

40–41 AUSTRALIA
National Geographic, insert on Australia, Washington, July 2000

World Heritage Sites: Unesco 2000 < www.unesco.org/whc>

Threatened Species and **Degree of Threat:** IUCN Red List 2000

42–43 CENTRAL AND SOUTH AMERICA
John Vidal, 'Road to Oblivion' *Guardian*, June 11, 2001, G2, p6, quoting William Laurence of Smithsonian Institute in *Science*, January 19, 2001

Monitoring of the Brazilian Amazonian Forest by Satellite 1998 to 1999, Instituto Nacional de Pesquisas Espaciais, April 2000

Protected Land: *World Resources 2000–2001*, WRI, 2000, Table BI.1

World Heritage Sites: <www.unesco.org/whc/nwhc/pages/sites/main.htm>

Amazon Basin: <www.unep-wcmc.org>

44–45 GALAPAGOS
Galapagos Conservation Trust <www.gct.org>

Galapagos Coalition <serv1.law.emory.edu/sites/GALAPAGOS/>

Darwin Foundation <www.darwinfoundation.org>

<www.wwf.org/galapagos/iguana.htm>

<www.geocities.com/RainForest/Jungle/7751/lavagull.html>

46–47 MADAGASCAR
Protected Areas: <www.wcmc.org.uk/cgi-bin/pa_paisquery.p>

Threatened Animals, Degree of Threat, Threatened Plant Species: <www.redlist.org>

Madagascar Rosy Periwinkle: <www.mobot.org>

<www.panda.org>

<www.lib.utexas.edu>

<www.chass.utoronto.ca/anthropology>

Part 4 ENDANGERED ANIMALS AND PLANTS

50–51 PRIMATES
P Day, "British Biologist Warns of Threat to Monkeys", *Daily Telegraph*, October 31, 1999, p16

Duke University Primate Center <www.duke.edu/web/primate>

G Lean & D Hinrichsen *Atlas of the Environment*, Helicon 1992

University of Manitoba <www.umanitoba.ca>

<www.columbia.edu/cu/pr/96_99/19244.html>

Threatened Primates: *2000 IUCN Red List of Threatened Species* <www.redlist.org/>

52–53 BIG CATS
<web.inter.nl.net/users/tiger/aboutset.html>

<www.snowleopard.org/facts.html>

<www.halcyon.com/mongolia/snowleopard.html>

Threatened Big Cats: *2000 IUCN Red List of Threatened Species*, <www.redlist.org>

Decline of the Tiger: Zoe Foundation

54–55 UNGULATES
Threatened Ungulates: *2000 IUCN Red List of Threatened Species*, <www.redlist.org>

Changing Fortunes of the North American Bison: <bisoncentral.com>

Wild Population of Arabian Oryx: <www.animalinfo.org/index.htm>

56–57 ELEPHANTS & RHINOS
Distribution of Elephants and Rhinos: *2000 IUCN Red List of Threatened Species* <www.redlist.org> International Rhino Foundation <www.rhinos-irf.org>

58–59 BEARS

Elizabeth Kemf, Alison Wilson and Christopher Servheen, *Bears in the Wild*, WWF, 1999
Threatened Bears and Threatened Pandas: *2000 IUCN Red List of Threatened Species* <www.redlist.org>
Population of Threatened Bears: <www.panda.org>

60–61 RODENTS

Ronald Nowak, *Walker's Mammals of the World*, 6th Edition, Vol II. Baltimore and London: The Johns Hopkins University Press, 1999
Threatened Rodents: *2000 IUCN Red List of Threatened Species* <www.redlist.org>
A Marmot on the Brink: A Bryant, *Forestry and historical population dynamics of the endangered Vancouver Island marmot*, Contributed talk, American Society of Mammalogists meeting, Durham, New Hampshire, June 2000 (courtesy of Marmot Recovery Foundation) <www.speciesatrisk.gc.ca>

62–63 BATS

Threatened Bats: *2000 IUCN Red List of Threatened Species*, IUCN – The WorldConservation Union, <www.redlist.org>

64–65 DOLPHINS AND WHALES

Threatened Dolphins and Whales: *2000 IUCN Red List of Threatened Species*, <www.redlist.org>
Great Whale Populations: International Whaling Commission <ourworld.compuserve.com/homepages/iwcoffice/Estimate.htm>

66–67 REPTILES AND AMPHIBIANS

Threatened Reptiles and Threatened Amphibians: *2000 IUCN Red List of Threatened Species*, <www.redlist.org>

68–69 INVERTEBRATES

Threatened Invertebrates and Threatened Crustaceans: *2000 IUCN Red List of Threatened Species* <www.redlist.org>

70–71 FISH

The State of World Fisheries and Aquaculture 2000, Food and Agriculture Organization Fisheries Department <www.fao.org/fi/default.asp>
Threatened Fish: *2000 IUCN Red List of Threatened Species* <www.redlist.org>
Increase in Fish Catch and Global Catch: FAO, 2001 <www.fao.org/fi/default.asp>

72–73 PLANTS

Threatened Plants and Extent of Threat: *1997 IUCN Red List of Threatened Plants* <www.redlist.org>

Part 5 Endangered Birds

76–77 BIRDS

Threatened Birds: *2000 IUCN Red List of Threatened Species* <www.redlist.org>
Bird species density: *World Resources 2000–2001*, Table BI.2
Farmland Birds: UK Farmland Bird Population Change: Royal Society for the Protection of Birds <www.rspb.org.uk>

78–79 BIRDS OF PREY

Threatened Birds of Prey: *2000 IUCN Red List of Threatened Species* <www.redlist.org>
Californian Condor in Crisis: US Fish & Wildlife Service, 1996, *Recovery Plan for the California Condor*
Decline of Asian White-backed Vulture: V Prakash, Bombay Natural History Society, quoted on: <www.peregrinefund.org/conserv_vulture. html>
Great Philippine eagle: < www.panda.org>

80–81 PARROTS AND COCKATOOS

N Snyder, P McGowan, J Gilardi and A Grajal, eds., 2000, *Parrots: Status Survey and Conservation Action Plan*. Species Survival Commission WWF < www.panda.org>
Threatened Parrots and Cockatoos: *2000 IUCN Red List of Threatened Species* <www.redlist.org>
Puerto Rican Amazon Parrot: C F Quist *et al*, *Granular cell tumor in an endangered Puerto Rican amazon parrot* <www.vet.uga.edu/IVCVM/1998/quist/quist.htm>
Yellow-eared Conure: <www.abcbirds.org/counterparts/project_yellow-eared_parrot.htm>

82–83 SEABIRDS

United Nations General Assembly Resolution 46-215, December 20, 1991
BirdLife International Seabird Conservation Programme: <www.uct.ac.za/depts/stats/adu/seabirds/>
<www.baheera.com/inthewild/vanishing.htm>
WWF < www.panda.org>
Threatened Seabirds: *2000 IUCN Red List of Threatened Species*
Spectacled petrel: <www.uct.ac.za/depts/stats/adu/seabirds/wbw/redbook.htm>

Short-tailed albatross: <www.uct.ac.za/depts/stats/adu/seabirds/>; personal communication from Hiroshi Hasegawa July 2001

84–85 MIGRATING BIRDS
<www.environment.gov.au/water/wetlands>
<www.panda.org/resources/publications/climate/migration/page5.htm>
<www.ramsar.org/key_montreux_record.htm>

Americas:
<north.audubon.org>
<birds.cornell.edu/bow/ruthum/>
<www.ecst.csuchico.edu/~tgeier/bird/pac.html>
<www.ankn.uaf.edu/units/birdslesson5.html>
<www.r5.fs.fed.us/hawk/html/fs_programs.htm>
<arnica.csustan.edu/esrpp/swainson.htm>
<www.panda.org>

Europe and Africa:
<orn-lab.ekol.lu.se/birdmigration/migrpatterns>
<www.birdwatchireland.ie>
Guardian Education March 28, 2000
<www.birds.org.il>
<www.terrestrialmap.org/TernWkrm.htm>
<www.wildwatch.com/backissues/feb2001/regulars/birds.htm>
<www.environment.gov.au/water/wetlands>
<www.zpok.hu/cyanide/baiamare/docs/donana.htm>
<marathonandmore.tripod.com/ornimalta-tourism.html>
<www.unesco.org/whc/nwhc/pages/sites/main.htm>

Asia and Oceania:
<www.environment.gov.au/water/wetlands>
<www.me.go.kr/english/sub/na_3.htm>
<www.tasweb.com.au/awsg/flyways.htm>
<www.environment.gov.au/water/wetlands/mwp/apstrat.htm#2.1thegeographicregion>
<www.wing-wbsj.or.jp/birdlife/asia_book/news_release.htm>
<www.sanctuaryasia.com/past_articles17.html>

Part 6 ISSUES OF CONSERVATION

88–89 ANIMAL BIODIVERSITY
B Groombridge and M D Jenkins, *Global Biodiversity*, World Conservation Press, 2000
Animal Biodiversity and **Total Known Species:** *World Resources 2000-2001* WRI, 2000, Table BI.3

90–91 PLANT BIODIVERSITY
B Groombridge and M D Jenkins, *Global Biodiversity*, World Conservation Press, 2000
Plant Biodiveristy: *World Resources 2000-2001* Table BI.3
Number of Plant Species: UNEP-WCMC

92–93 ECOLOGICAL HOTSPOTS
Conservation Focus: Conservation International <www.conservation.org/Hotspots/>; WWF <www.worldwildlife.org/global200/> <www.nationalgeographic.com/wildworld/global.htm>

94–95 CONSERVING ANIMALS
Conservation Zoos: <www.cbsg.org> <www.goodzoos.com/conserva.htm>
Amur leopard: <amur-leopard.org>
Fall and Rise of the Nene: <www.wwt.org.uk>

96–97 CONSERVING PLANTS
<www.nps.gov/plants/index.htm>
Plant Research Centers: <www.nybg.org/bsci/ih/>
Kew Gardens: <www.rbgkew.org.uk>
Golden Pagoda: <www.redlist.org>

98–99 CONSERVING DOMESTIC BREEDS
<www.new-agri.co.uk/01-1/focuson/focuson3.html>
Threatened Domestic Breeds: FAO, *World Watch Lists for Domestic Animal Diversity*, FAO 2000

100–101 IMPORT TRADE
<www. cites.org>
Major Importers: *World Resources 2000–2001*, WRI, 2000 Table BI.4
Rhino horn: <www.iss.co.za/pubs/asr/6.1/du%20bois.html>
Orang-utan: A Cronin, *Ape Rescue Chronicle* Summer 2000, <www.monkeyworld.org>

102–103 EXPORT TRADE
Major Exporters: *World Resources 2000–2001*, WRI, 2000 Table BI.4
Sturgeon ban: <www.cites.org/eng/newsl>
Ivory: <www. cites.org>

INDEX

Figures in **bold** indicate a map, chart, graph, picture or text on map. Only countries mentioned in the main text are indexed.